GREAT AMERICAN ARTISTS for Kids

2nd Edition

Hands–On Art Experiences in the Styles of Great American Masters

MaryAnn F. Kohl & Kim Solga

CHICAGO REVIEW PRESS

Copyright © 2008, 2019 by MaryAnn F. Kohl and Kim Solga
All rights reserved
Published by Chicago Review Press Incorporated
814 North Franklin Street
Chicago, Illinois 60610
ISBN 978-1-64160-170-2

Disclaimer: The publisher, Chicago Review Press Inc., and the authors, MaryAnn F. Kohl and Kim Solga, affirm that children must be supervised by an adult at all times while involved in the art activities found in *Great American Artists for Kids*. Guidance for proper use of art materials must be strictly followed at all times. It is crucial that caution be observed at all times and that the abilities of children involved be assessed according to appropriateness or developmental level to safely engage in activities from *Great American Artists for Kids*.The publisher and the authors assume no responsibility or liability whatsoever for activities in this book, nor for adult supervision, nor for any use of art materials by or with children.

The Frank Lloyd Wright name, likeness and associated publicity rights, the Frank Lloyd Wright ® mark and variations thereof, are all the property of The Frank Lloyd Wright Foundation, Taliesin West, Scottsdale, AZ. All drawings and designs of Mr. Wright protected under Copyright. © 2008, Frank Lloyd Wright Foundation / Artists Rights Society (ARS), New York.

Library of Congress Cataloging-in-Publication Data
Names: Kohl, MaryAnn F., author. | Solga, Kim, author.
Title: Great American artists for kids : hands-on art experiences in the
    styles of great American masters / MaryAnn F. Kohl, Kim Solga.
Description: Chicago, Illinois : Chicago Review Press, 2019. | Includes
    index. | Audience: Ages 4-12. | Audience: K to Grade 3.
Identifiers: LCCN 2019005128| ISBN 9781641601702 (paperback) | ISBN
    9781641601726 (kindle) | ISBN 9781641601733 (epub)
Subjects: LCSH: Art—Technique—Juvenile literature. | Art,
    American—Juvenile literature. | BISAC: JUVENILE NONFICTION / Games &
    Activities / General. | JUVENILE NONFICTION / Art / General.
Classification: LCC N7430 .K597 2019 | DDC 709.73—dc23 LC record available at https://lccn.loc.
gov/2019005128

Cover design: Lindsey Schauer
Cover photographs: *Frank Lloyd Wright Triptych* © 2018 Frank Lloyd Wright Foundation. All Rights
    Reserved. Licensed by Artists Rights Society; *I...I'm Sorry!* © Estate of Roy Lichtenstein; *Mrs.
    Joshua Montgomery Sears*, John Singer Sargent, Museum of Fine Arts, Houston, Texas, USA
    Museum purchase funded by George R. Brown in honor of his wife, Alice Pratt Brown/Bridgeman
Interior design: Jonathan Hahn

Printed in the United States of America
5 4 3 2 1

Dedication and Appreciation

Jennifer Jo Martens Stickney

September 30, 1971–September 8, 2007

JJ brightened the life of every person who ever met her. There will be no forgetting this beautiful woman—her smile, her positive outlook, and her joy for life.

This book—full of color and joyful creativity and fun—is for JJ.

Photograph by Jon Stickney, courtesy of Jon Stickney and Patrick Martens

Words of Appreciation

Special thanks and deepest appreciation go to all the children, artists, museums, teachers, friends, and coworkers who enthusiastically joined in and made *Great American Artists for Kids* possible. Each of you is an important part of this book. Thank you, thank you.

- All the young artists who enthusiastically tested and perfected activities and shared their wonderful creations. Special thanks to Mrs. Van Slyke's second grade class at Bernice Vosbeck Elementary School, Lynden, Washington, who worked side by side with the authors creating artwork, meeting deadlines, and supplying endless enthusiasm. This book would not exist without each of you! Names of all young artists with page numbers of their art images can be found on pp. 130.

- Artists, museums, galleries, foundations, and estates who saw their way to graciously and generously share art images with young artists through this book.

- Michael Kohl, for support through several computer crashes, long work days, great ideas for art activities and cover, and for starting mornings with muffins and tea.

- Ned Harkness and Ariana Moulton, ultra-creative teachers at Lincoln Elementary School, Chicago, for organizing the Grant Wood Art Focus. Thanks to all of their students, too!

- Candy Ford, newly "retired" grade two teacher and friend, for keeping permissions and credits organized between travels to sunny places.

- Carol Sabbeth, author of *Monet and the Impressionists for Kids*, for generously sharing art-author experiences, and putting us on the right track to finding permissions for art images.

- Friends and coworkers Kathy Charner, Cathy Calliotte, Larry Rood, Leah Curry-Rood, and Mark Voigt for their unfailing support now, in the past, and forevermore.

- Thanks once more to each great American artist or artist's representative who generously contributed to the success of this book.

Icon Guide

Experience, Prep/Plan, and Art Technique Icons

Icons are positioned in the upper corner of each art activity page to assist a parent, teacher, or young artist with evaluating the attributes or materials of an art activity. Icons help make choosing an art project quick and easy.

Child Experience Icon

Because age and skill do not necessarily go hand in hand, the starred Experience Icons indicate projects that are easiest, moderate, or most involved for children. All children are welcome and encouraged to experience all projects regardless of their skill levels. Beginning artists will need more help or supervision with involved projects. More advanced artists will work independently on easier projects. Use these icons as guides, not rules.

 One Star for beginning artists with little experience (easiest art activity)

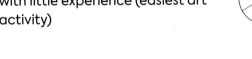 **Two Stars** for artists with some experience and moderate skill (intermediate art activity)

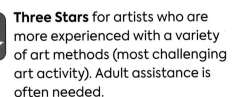 **Three Stars** for artists who are more experienced with a variety of art methods (most challenging art activity). Adult assistance is often needed.

Adult Plan and Prep Icon

The planning and preparation icon indicates the degree of involvement and time expected for the adult in charge, ranging from quick or little involvement/planning, to moderate involvement/planning, to significant involvement/planning.

 Little adult planning and preparation

 Moderate adult planning and preparation

 Involved adult planning and preparation

Art Technique Icon

Art icons help the reader quickly assess the key art technique or materials that are the focus of the activity. When activities have more than one technique, the main one will be listed first, followed by others.

Draw

Paint

Cut/Collage

Glue

Print

Clay

Mixture/Dough

Craft/Construct

Sew/Weave

Tape/Assemble

Computer

Chalk

Photography/Camera

Sculpture

Artist Style Icon

In the art world and museums, great American artists from the past and present are often grouped into descriptive movements, styles, or eras. Definitions of these can be found in the glossary. Some artists are found grouped under more than one style and still others are difficult to place in any one particular style. When an artist fits into more than one category, more than one icon may be given. Take your time learning and remembering these categories. It can take years of exploration, discovery, study, and observation to get comfortable with all the classifications! For now, they are presented for the curious art explorers who wish to know more and to help categorize the unique styles of each great American artist. The more that artists and their techniques are explored, the easier it is to see how they fit into categories. Let the journey be one of enjoyment, discovery, and creativity.

 Abstract

 Abstract Expressionist, Post-Abstract Expressionist

 Architect

 Cartoonist

 Concept Artist

 Constructionist

 Expressionist, Neo-Expressionist

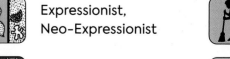 Fiber Artist/Quilter

 Folk Artist

 Funk Artist

 Glass Artist

 Graffiti Artist

 Illustrator

 Impressionist

 Installation Artist

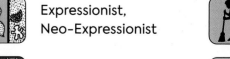 Land Artist

 Minimalist

 Naturalist

 Photographer

 Photorealist

 Pop Artist

 Potter

 Precisionist

 Printmaker

 Realist

 Regionalist

 Romanticist

 Surrealist

 Park Designer

Carver

Contents

 Early American Art

 New American Ideas

3 American Art Explodes

4 American Art Onward

Introduction

Great American Artists for Kids offers children hands-on activities to explore the styles and techniques of America's greatest artists, from colonial times to the present day. Each art process focuses on one style and one artist. A brief biography and portrait of each artist adds depth and interest to the art project. An option for very young children is offered for most activities. All young artists will create their own artworks using a technique or material that reflects the work of the great master. The most important aspects of the activities are exploration, discovery, and individual creativity.

Great American Artists for Kids introduces children to the masters of American art. Many great artists will have familiar names, like Cassatt, Warhol, and O'Keeffe. Other names may be new, such as Asawa, Smithson, and Magee. Each featured artist has a style that is accessible to children, and a life history that will inspire and interest them. The selection of these 75 artists from hundreds of greats was based on artists whose styles, histories, techniques, and artworks appeal to children of all ages. Many artists could not be included, but they are not forgotten! The companion book, *Discovering Great Artists*, has 100 artists to explore, many of whom are American. We hope you enjoy researching them all and seek out those artists who were not included in this volume. Perhaps you'll see them in one of our new books in the future. Visit www.brightring.com for links to artists from all over the world.

This is a book of exploration. Young children are more often interested in the process of art than in their finished product. They may or may not show interest in the related art history or art appreciation. But they will be soaking up the information! Many will be curious and eager to know more about an artist's life, what the artist's world was like, and how it influenced or inspired the artist's style. The information on each page is offered as a reference and inspiration for learners. Don't be surprised if children begin to collect knowledge about different artists and styles of art the way they collect baseball cards or dinosaur statistics.

Elementary school students from ASFM, the American School Foundation of Monterrey, Mexico, proudly show their individual art inspired by the works and lives of great American artists.

Mountain Lake by Nathan Johnston, 11, Inspired by William Sidney Mount, p. 20

Robot Appliqué by Raymond Unger, 9, Inspired by Harriet Powers, p. 14

Introduction

Hairy Monster by Enzo Greco, 4, Inspired by Harriet Powers, p. 26 © Lizette Greco 2005

Voom Car by Irina Ammasova, 8, Inspired by Roy Lichtenstein, p. 84

Great American Artists for Kids encourages kids to learn from doing as they become familiar with new ideas. If a child experiences composing a painting with the bleached-bone and desert-landscape shapes of Georgia O'Keeffe, then that child will feel more comfortable as an older student studying O'Keeffe's works. Imagine visiting the Museum of Modern Art in New York City and seeing in person those same works by O'Keeffe! Many children have expressed that it's like meeting an old friend.

The activities are open-ended. Most important for children is exploring new art ideas and techniques, celebrating their own unique art styles, abilities, and interests. It is up to each young artist to decide exactly how his or her work of art will turn out and what direction it will take. Independent thinking is encouraged, differences are celebrated as skills, and responsibility is enhanced through individual decisions.

Great American Artists for Kids has been carefully organized and presented to make its use easy, quick, inspiring, and useful. It is divided into chapters in which artists are grouped by the years they have been most artistically active. The chapters are color-coded so that flipping through the book becomes a comfortable way to find artists, art activities, or artworks by style or technique. The icons are also color-coded, as is the chart of contents. Most artists' pages show an original piece by the artist or a child's fine work in the artist's style. When an artist's work is not shown, a website is given where art may be readily seen. A full list of Internet sites is offered for viewing all artists' works in the resource guide, page 115. The index has just about everything you can think of, including listings by artists' names, art activity names, and art materials. Last but not least, the artists' birthdays are listed in the resource guide to assist in planning art celebrations, learning, and just plain fun.

These art activities will expand the creative experience and awareness of children in all aspects of the visual arts through painting, drawing , printmaking, sculpture, photography, and many other experiences with art materials. The activities in this book are for all ages and abilities, from the most basic skill level to the most challenging. Repeat projects often and discover new outcomes and learnings each time. Repetition brings comfort with art process and surprising growth in art technique and skills.

Great American Artists for Kids also encourages children to read books, visit museums and libraries, use the Internet, collect information, and look at the world in new ways. They will begin to encompass a greater sense of history and art appreciation while seeing their world in new perspective. Perhaps they will be inspired to carry art in their hearts as they grow and develop. They are already great artists in every sense of the word.

Early American Art

John James Audubon, *American Flamingo*
Phoenicopterus Ruber, Florida Keys, 1832
John Audubon image © visipix.com

Flamingo Reflection, by second grade student

John Singleton Copley

John Singleton Copley | *Watson and the Shark*, 1778
Oil on canvas, 91.4 × 77.5 cm, National Gallery of Art,
Ferdinand Lammot Belin Fund 1963.6.1, Washington, DC

July 3, 1738–September 9, 1815
Realist painter, Narrative, Portrait

John Singleton Copley [KOP-lee] was born in the colonial city of Boston in the years before the United States was an independent country. He taught himself how to paint and became Boston's most popular portrait artist. Portraits were a fine way for an artist to make a living because rich people paid top dollar to have an artist paint their pictures. Copley created many portraits of Boston's wealthiest families. One of his most famous portraits is of the patriot Paul Revere. Copley was very good at portraits, but he really loved to make paintings showing thrilling moments in history. In 1774, he moved to England and began to specialize in historical drama. He painted battle scenes and great sea victories. His best-known painting, *Watson and the Shark*, shows the true story of sailors trying to rescue a young swimmer from a hungry shark. Copley painted the most dramatic moment of the rescue, when the boatman is about to spear the shark as it surges toward the floundering boy. People viewing the painting have no way to tell if the boy will be saved or will be captured by the shark. The true ending of the story is that young Watson was rescued and grew up to be mayor of London at the time Copley lived there.

Narrative Drama

Copley's art tells stories. A picture that tells a story is called a narrative. Before cameras were invented, pictures were drawn of an event from reports by people who were witnesses. Draw a narrative picture, choosing a dramatic event. The story can be a true event or imagined.

Materials

white 9-by-12-inch drawing paper
pencil and eraser
for inspiration: news magazines, newspapers
choice of coloring tools: paints, colored pencils, watercolor pencils, markers, or crayons

Process

1. Select a dramatic event to illustrate: a true event, perhaps a recent story from a newspaper, or an imaginary event. A rescue is the perfect subject to capture the spirit of Copley's famous painting, *Watson and the Shark*. Possible ideas include:

   - fire fighters saving people from a burning building
   - lifeguards trying to reach a swimmer through crashing ocean waves
   - search-and-rescue team finding an injured hiker
   - rock climbers rescuing a fallen climber who is clinging to dangerous rocks

❷ Draw the scene from imagination, focusing on elements that tell the story. Try to imagine the scene as it really happened if true, or might have happened if imaginary. Choose what parts of the story to include in the drawing and what to leave out. Sketch with a pencil and eraser, and feel free to add elements that make the picture more dramatic. Zoom in on the action. Draw the people up close and fill the drawing paper edge-to-edge. Idea for detail: Use the Internet to find photos of equipment, see what a firefighter uniform looks like, or learn how a climbing rope attaches to a rock climber.

❸ Color the drawing with a choice of paints, colored pencils, water-color pencils, markers, or crayons.

❹ Idea for Expression: Use color contrast to make the drawing more interesting, spooky, or dramatic. To do this, color the center of the action with bright colors, while making the background dark and shadowy.

Run, Little Deer, Run!, by Eva Thomas, 5

Eva describes her dramatic narrative art saying, "See the little purple bird? He's helping the deer escape from the dangerous forest fire."

Car Crash, by Sierra Smith, 7

Thomas Jefferson

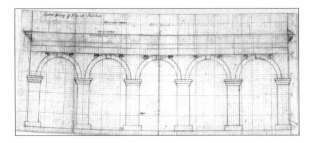

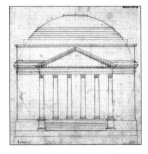 

April 13, 1743–July 4, 1826
Architect, Classical

Thomas Jefferson [JEF-er-sun] was an influential Founding Father of the United States of America, the third president of the United States (1801–1809), and the leading author of the Declaration of Independence (1776). Architecture was Jefferson's favorite thing. He collected a private library of books about architecture and taught himself about Greek and Roman classical buildings. The keystone arch was one of his favorite design features. Some fun things to know about Jefferson: he washed his feet every morning in cold water to prevent colds, he was over six feet tall with red hair, he could read seven languages, and he once had a pet mockingbird. Jefferson died on the fourth of July in 1826, and many years later in 1993, he was honored with the American Institute of Architects Gold Medal.

Thomas Jefferson | *Study for south elevation of Pavilion VII lower portico*, before 1817?
Pricking, scoring and iron gall ink, Engraved graph paper, 6 × 15 in | Jefferson, ViU, N307, K No. 3, L-07-02, L-07-03 | Permission from the Department of Architectural History, University of Virginia.

Clay Keystone Arch

The arch is a way of making a roof, doorway, or window using only clay bricks or blocks of wood or stone. The weight of the blocks holds the arch together without beams, cement, glue, or tape. To experiment with this phenomenon, build a keystone arch with play clay. The "key" stone will make the arch stand. Add more walls and windows to expand this architectural experience.

Materials

play clay, Plasticine, or other clays
plastic placemat or a large sheet of paper
assortment of clay tools: ruler, hammer, plastic
    knife, toothpick, rolling pin, bamboo skewer
optional building materials: wooden building
    blocks, marshmallows, cardboard boxes, milk
    cartons

Process

❶ Form clay into small bricks about 1- to 2-inches square. Make about 20 blocks, all the same size. More can be made, but 20 is a good number to begin.

❷ Stack five to nine of the blocks in a column that balances nicely.

❸ Stack an equal number of blocks into a second column a few inches away from the first.

❹ Now for the magic moment that Jefferson loved! Form one keystone block that is slightly smaller at the bottom and larger at the top. Hold the keystone between the columns. Slowly lean the two columns inward toward each other, holding the keystone between them. Let the columns touch the keystone. Let go! Do the two columns form an arch that stands alone? If not, try again. It will work with a few more attempts. Try higher or lower columns, and larger or smaller bricks. This is an experiment, which means trying different ideas is important and interesting.

❺ When the two columns meet in a curve and stand alone, the keystone arch is a success.

❻ Continue building more walls, doors, or windows, if desired. Add a cardboard roof. Think of other features to add, like a flagpole and flag, sidewalk, or courtyard.

Gilbert Stuart

December 3, 1755–June 9, 1828
Realist painter, Portrait

Gilbert Stuart [STOO-ert] grew up in the American colony of Rhode Island before the United States was an independent nation. He traveled to Scotland, England, and Ireland to study art. He then returned to America about the time the war for independence broke out, but he returned to Europe once again because the war made his career as an artist difficult. Even so, he didn't find much success until he came back to the United States in 1795, when he painted a portrait of George Washington. The portrait soon became famous, and the demand for copies and new paintings kept Stuart very busy. Stuart is called the "father of American portraiture" because he painted pictures of all the famous people of early America. One of his paintings of George Washington was hung in the White House. During the War of 1812, the British burned the White House, but First Lady Dolly Madison rescued the painting before it went up in flames. Today, this painting still hangs in the East Room of the White House. The image of Washington on the US dollar bill came from one of Stuart's most famous paintings of Washington.

Gilbert Stuart | *Mrs. Harrison Gray Otis (Sally Foster Otis)*, 1809
Oil on mahogany panel, 32 × 26 in | Reynolda House Museum of
American Art, Winston-Salem, North Carolina

Painted Crackle Crayon

Stuart's portrait paintings are now 200 years old, and the smooth, glossy oil paints he used have dried and aged, showing antique texture cracks. To approximate a crackled antique appearance, draw a portrait on manila paper with crayons. Gently crumple the portrait into a ball, then open and flatten it, causing cracks and creases. Paint over the portrait with a thin black wash.

Materials

manila paper, 9 by 12 inches
crayons
paint wash: black tempera paint, thinned with water
2 soft paintbrushes
white glue, slightly thinned with water
construction paper, larger than manila paper (optional)

Process

1. Draw a picture portrait of someone's face. Draw and color heavily with crayon, covering the manila paper with thick crayon color.
2. When the portrait is done, gently crumple the paper into a little ball. Squeeze it and press on it to get a very wrinkled ball of paper. Then carefully open and flatten the paper on the work surface.
3. To create the cracked design, brush the black paint wash over the crayon work. A thin wash works best. (Any dark color will work in place of black.) The paint will go into all the little cracks that appeared when the paper was crumpled, but it won't stick to the waxy crayon. Let the artwork dry.
4. Once dry, a coating of slightly thinned white glue can be brushed onto the portrait to give it a little shine. Dry overnight.
5. The completed crackle design may be further glued or taped to a larger sheet of colored paper to give it added weight and a colorful framed edge.

Cracked Crayon Portrait,
by Ashely, 8

Edward Hicks

And not one savage beast be seen to frown.

His grim carnivrous nature then shall cease.

A little child shall lead them on in love.

When man is led and moved by sovereign grace.

Edward Hicks | *Peaceable Kingdom of the Branch*, c.1826
Oil on canvas, 23½ × 30¾ in | Gift of Barbara B. Millhouse, Reynolda
House Museum of American Art, Winston-Salem, North Carolina

April 4, 1780–August 23, 1849
Folk art painter

Edward Hicks [hiks] was born in Pennsylvania just a few years after the United States became an independent nation. He grew up on his father's farm. As a young man, he became an apprentice coachmaker and used his artistic abilities by painting designs on the coaches and signs for many of the businesses in his town. When Hicks became a Quaker, a peaceful and conservative religion, he gave up painting and for many years was a traveling preacher in the northern US and Canada. He later decided that a good Quaker must earn a living, and because painting was one of his skills, he returned to creating art with a message. He believed deeply in peaceful cooperation, and his paintings express this spiritual message over and over. Hick's most famous work is titled *The Peaceable Kingdom*. He made nearly 100 paintings with this same title. The paintings show animals who are natural enemies lying down peacefully together: a lion rests next to a lamb, predators sit gently with their prey, little children walk unharmed among wild animals. His paintings have a moral message that helps people understand they could live peacefully together.

Peaceable Collage

Find animals in magazine pictures that are natural enemies in the wild. Clip and assemble these and other collage materials in a simple, peaceful collage.

Materials

sheet of heavy paper or posterboard

magazines with wildlife photos

scissors

white glue or glue stick

any additional collage materials: crayons, markers, leaves, grass, yarn, small fabric scraps, sequins, glitter, colored paper scraps, foil, dry rice or beans, sand, sewing trims, lace, buttons

Process

1. Look through magazines for photos of animals that are natural enemies or "predator and prey." Some possible choices are: the arctic wolf and caribou, owl and field mouse, lion and zebra, or shark and colorful coral reef fish.

2. Cut out each animal picture chosen, cutting around the animal shapes following the edges of their bodies.

3. Arrange the prey and predator pictures on white paper or posterboard in any design. Glue the pictures in place.

4. A collage is a design made from many different elements, so now add any coloring, outlining, decorations, papers, or other materials and items to finish the collage. Glue and color until satisfied. The finished artwork will show animals together in a peaceful design.

Pacific Northwest Peace Rally, by Morgan Van Slyke, 12

Peaceable Snow Leopard with Rodents, by Cedar Kirwin, 12

Hawk with Hamster and Friends, by Julia Odegaard, 10

John James Audubon

John James Audubon | *Blue Jay*, 1785–1851

The Birds of America: From Original Drawings; reissued by J. W. Audubon; chromolithography by J. Bien. New York: Roe Lockwood & Son, 1860. Photo courtesy of University of Delaware Library, Newark, Delaware

April 26, 1785–January 27, 1851
Realist painter, Naturalist

John James Audubon [AW-duh-bahn] set a goal to paint every kind of bird in North America and to do it by observing real birds in the fields and forests where they lived. The paintings he created are the most famous pictures of birds in the world. Audubon was born on an island in the Caribbean. He grew up in France, then he moved to the United States as a young man. He was interested in the natural history of birds, how they behaved, and where they lived. He spent much of his time roaming and painting in the outdoors, but he was a good businessman, too. He took his paintings to Europe and had them made into fine prints to sell to collectors. Audubon's book, *Birds of America*, filled with large, hand-colored engravings of birds, has been called the greatest picture book ever made. Audubon's art shows birds in their natural habitats. He traveled through the wilderness to find new species to capture and paint. His work took him from the swamps of Florida to the ice of northern Canada, and his dedication to excellence made John James Audubon one of the best-known American artists of all.

Nici Smith, 11, sketches bugs and critters in the wild. Mt. Shasta, California
Photograph by Kim Solga

Draw Bugs 'n' Critters

Adult supervision required

John James Audubon observed real birds as models for his paintings. He drew birds in their natural settings, active and true to life. Explore Audubon's techniques by drawing a living creature like a bug or animal found in your area.

Materials

a living bug or other critter
handheld magnifying glass
small clear jar
aluminum foil for lid
tool to poke holes in foil, such as
   an opened paper clip

drawing paper
pencils and eraser
choice of coloring tools: colored
   pencils, crayons, charcoal,
   chalk, marking pens,
   watercolors

Process

Draw Bugs

❶ It's easy to find an insect model to draw, especially during warm summer months. Bugs are everywhere: moths circling the porch light, ants crawling on the sidewalk, ladybugs and beetles flying in the garden. Place the insect in a small clear jar covered tightly with aluminum foil. Poke tiny holes in the foil to let in air. Bugs will be released unharmed at the end of the project. Adult supervision is required.

❷ Drawing a living bug is an adventure in observation. A handheld magnifying glass is great for seeing details. Look closely. Notice the bug's colors and shapes, how the legs move, the appearance of wings and antennae and eyes. Work big! Lightly sketch its outline on paper, making the picture much larger than the actual bug.

❸ Draw each part of the bug, looking at the living model to draw every detail as realistically as possible.

❹ Color the drawing with colored pencils, markers, or crayons, or use watercolors and a fine-tip paintbrush.

❺ Audubon liked to name his art and provide dates or other details. Do the same with a pencil or pen, if desired.

❻ When the drawing is complete, return the bug to the place where it was caught so it can continue with its life, unharmed.

Draw Critters

Other living creatures can be drawn in detail as well. Following are some suggestions. All shoud be observed or captured safely and released with your adult helper.

- lizard
- frog
- dog
- cat
- parakeet
- parrot

- gerbil
- hamster
- guinea pig
- rabbit
- fish

Real Live Bug,
by Juliana Crews, 4

Lizard Detail,
by Mark, 11

Frederic Remington

October 4, 1861–December 26, 1909
Realist sculptor, painter

When he was a boy growing up in New York, Frederic Remington [REM-ing-tuhn] liked to draw pictures of firefighters, soldiers, heroes, and adventurous people. He grew up to draw, paint, and sculpt the heroes of the American West, and he became the most famous of all cowboy artists. The American West was a thrilling land to visit in 1881 when young Remington first left the city and traveled to the wild frontier of the Montana Territory. He sketched the scenery and people he met in his travels. Remington sold his drawings to publishers in the East, where newspapers and magazines were thrilled to receive such exciting illustrations. Remington returned to the East and a studio in New York filled with a huge collection of Western souvenirs and cowboy clothing. Here Remington painted romantic pictures of colorful trappers, cavalry, bronco-busters, and Native American braves. He learned how to make bronze statues of his art by pouring molten metal into a hollow mold, a process that allowed him to make hundreds of bronze copies of a single sculpture. His bronze statues of cowboys and horses are his most famous works. Although Remington did not live a long life, he was a hardworking, successful artist who created thousands of works of art celebrating the American West.

Frederic Remington | *The Wicked Pony*, 1904
Courtesy of Special Collections/Musselman Library,
Gettysburg College, Gettysburg, Pennsylvania

Frederic Remington | *The Stampede*, 1909
Courtesy of Special Collections/Musselman Library,
Gettysburg College, Gettysburg, Pennsylvania

Face Casting

Adult supervision required

Remington created bronze statues by making a clay sculpture first, an art process called "casting." Polymer clay and Plaster of Paris will take the place of Remington's clay and molten bronze materials. The artist can make a casting of a face in this sculpture project.

Materials

1 to 2 pounds of polymer clay, such as Sculpey or Fimo
Plaster of Paris (found at a hardware or hobby store)
water and container for mixing plaster
small sticks and other small tools to shape the clay
choice of decorating materials: markers, acrylic paints and
  paintbrush

Process

❶ Start with a small lump of polymer clay about the size of a lemon. Squeeze it to soften. Push the lump onto a table and shape it into a face. Think of a face to make such as a monster, superhero, princess, cat, owl, any face at all. Poke and pinch the clay to make a nose, eyes, lips, and hair. Use small tools to poke and carve textures and details into the clay.

❷ Have an adult bake the clay face sculpture following the instructions on the polymer clay box. Then let it cool completely after baking.

❸ The casting part of this project starts once the face sculpture is baked and hardened. Now it is time to make a mold of the face sculpture, then cast a copy of it. To do this, take a large chunk of polymer clay and flatten it into a brick shape that is 2 inches wider and taller than the face sculpture, and is about 3 inches thick.

❹ Gently press the face sculpture, face down, into the soft clay brick. Push slowly and firmly, maybe wiggling it a bit so the face buries itself in the soft clay. Then carefully lift it out. What's left behind is a mold of the face sculpture—a hollow that is exactly the shape of the sculpted and baked face.

❺ Stir water slowly into about ½ cup of Plaster of Paris in a container until thick like a milkshake. (An adult should supervise so the child does not breathe the plaster powder.) Pour wet plaster into the hollow mold in the clay,and let it sit still. The plaster will harden and become strong in an hour or two. (Place any leftover plaster in a plastic bag in the trash. Do NOT RINSE PLASTER DOWN THE DRAIN or it may seriously clog plumbing!)

❻ Bend the clay mold to remove the plaster casting. It will be damp and fragile and must now dry overnight. (Note: If the hardened plaster was carefully removed, another batch of wet plaster may be poured into the same hollow mold and another casting made—even 100 cast copies of the face could be made!) Face castings may be painted or decorated with markers. If several castings were made, they can be made to look identical or each can be made completely unique.

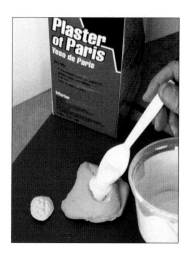

Mary Cassatt

Mary Cassatt | *Madame Gaillard and Her Daughter Marie-Thérèse*, 1897
Pastel on paper, 23 × 28¾ in, Gift of Barbara B. Millhouse, Reynolda House Museum of American Art, Winston-Salem, North Carolina

May 23, 1844–June 14, 1926
Impressionist painter, Printmaker

Mary Cassatt [kuh-SAHT] was born in Pennsylvania, the fourth of five children born in her well-to-do family. Mary Cassatt and her family traveled throughout Europe and visited many countries by the time she was 10. In those days, most wealthy women did not have professions, and there were very few women artists. Her family did not approve when she decided to become an artist, but her desire was so strong, she bravely took the steps to make art her career. She studied first in Philadelphia, and then went to Paris to study painting. She admired the work of Edgar Degas and was able to meet him, which was a great inspiration. Her parents thought she should not be living alone in Paris, so they went to live with her, bringing her sister Lydia with them. Even though Lydia became very ill and her parents were growing older and needed care, she still found time to paint. Though she never had children of her own, she loved children and painted portraits of the children of her friends and family. She became known as the painter of mothers and children. Cassatt lost her sight at the age of 70 and, sadly, was not able to paint during the later years of her life. She retired to her French country estate. Mary Cassatt will be remembered as a great American artist and a brave, independent woman.

Monoprint Back-Draw

Create a back-draw monoprint by spreading paint smoothly on a flat surface and then lightly placing paper on the paint. Draw firmly and directly on the paper with a pencil. Lift the paper to reveal the monoprint on the reverse side of the paper. Many of Cassatt's artworks were called monoprints or monotypes, which means one print was made from a painting of ink or paint on a printing surface or plate.

Materials

choice of paint, liquid acrylic or tempera
smooth surface, such as a countertop, cookie sheet, or sheet of Plexiglas
brayer to roll paint or a wide sponge brush
several sheets of copier paper
pencil, pen, or crayon

Process

1. Squirt some paint on the smooth surface. Roll it thin and even with a brayer to about the same size as the paper. If a brayer is not available, use a sponge brush to brush the paint as smoothly and evenly as possible. The smoother, the better. A few drops of water can be added if the paint starts to dry out too quickly.
2. Gently and quickly place a sheet of copier paper on the painted area. (The paper can be dampened slightly to help it accept the paint.)
3. Pressing firmly, draw with a pencil, pen, or crayon. Draw quickly and firmly. Pat gently around the drawing to pick up more paint.
4. Lift and peel the paper from the paint and see the image that has been transferred to the paper. Notice how the drawing tool plowed a groove through the paint to give an interesting double-line effect.

Moms and Babies, by Jalani Phelps, 8

5. Depending on how the monoprint turned out, additional monoprints can be created:
   - If the first print was thick and hard to see, do not add more paint. Roll the paint smooth again, and then proceed to make a new back-draw monoprint with a fresh sheet of paper and a new drawing.
   - If the first print was too light, add more paint and maybe a few drops of water, roll smooth again, and make a new drawing and print.

Harriet Powers

Harriet Power | *Bible Quilt*, 1886
#75-2984, National Museum of American History, Smithsonian Institution, Washington, DC

October 29, 1837–January 1, 1910
Fiber Artist, Quilter

Harriet Powers [POW-erz] was born in slavery near Athens, Georgia. Years later, as a free woman, she created two quilts thought to be the best of their kind anywhere in the entire world. Powers used a traditional African appliqué technique to record important events and ideas on her quilts, a source for telling stories. She often included local legends, Bible stories, and heavenly events. When she was 49 years old, Powers began to exhibit her quilts. A southern artist named Jennie Smith saw them at a craft fair. Powers didn't want to sell them but later changed her mind. Smith said that Powers would visit her quilts because they were so precious to her. Because Harriet Powers agreed to sell her quilts, she has preserved them for future generations to treasure. They are now on display in the Smithsonian Museum of Art in Washington, DC.

Felt Appliqué

Create an easy, bright, bold appliqué with sticky-backed hobby felt. No sewing is needed, though stitching with yarn adds to the true appliqué experience. Further decorate with sewing trims, buttons, and fabric scraps. The art can tell a story or simply fill a wall with color.

Note about sewing: Many children are capable of sewing with a sewing machine with adult assistance. Practice first on scraps and begin slowly.

Hairy Monster, Original drawing by Enzo Greco, 4.
Construction for shoulder bag by Lizette Greco. © Lizette Greco 2005

Materials

craft felt with sticky backing, several small sheets in different colors
large piece of felt for background
scissors
yarn and large darning needle

choice of decorating materials: buttons, sequins, faux fur, fabric scraps, sewing trims, felt scraps
fabric glue
sewing machine (optional)
display materials (optional): cardboard, wood, stapler

Process

1. Think of a picture or design to create with pieces of felt. The picture could tell a story, hold a memory of an event, or may simply be a picture that stands alone. Sewing pieces to a larger fabric to make a picture is called an appliqué.
2. Draw the different parts of the picture on sticky-backed craft felt squares with a marker. Cut out the pieces. Stick the pieces to the large piece of felt, assembling them into a picture.
3. To add more design and interest, sew through the design with yarn on a large needle. Use a large "in and out" stitch with colorful yarn about 12- to 24-inches in length.
4. Sew or glue on more decorations, buttons, and sewing trims. Faux fur adds humor and design to people, animals, or creatures. Sequins add sparkle, and buttons look like eyes, lights, or push-buttons. Consider sewing decorations and shapes with a sewing machine with adult help.
5. To display the appliqué, pin it to a wall or a piece of cardboard. For a more polished look, attach the appliqué to a wood panel. Place the appliqué face down on the workspace. Center a piece of wood (4 inches smaller than the art) over the appliqué. Wrap the edges of the appliqué tightly back over the edges of the wood. Staple wrapped edges to the back to hold.

Currier & Ives

Currier: March 27, 1813–November 20, 1888
Ives: March 5, 1824–January 3, 1895
Illustrator, Printmaker, Romantic

Currier and Ives [KUR-ee-er] [EYEvz], a New York printing company, created artworks of popular scenes like sports, disasters, charming landscapes, patriotic events, and current happenings in the news. Nathaniel Currier started the company with a new printing method called lithography, beginning when he drew a picture of a famous building burning in a dramatic fire. He made prints and sold them just days after the fire occurred. Photography wasn't invented yet, so people were interested to see a picture of the actual event. Soon Currier was printing scenes of other events: boxing matches, a steamship burning on the ocean, parties, and sleigh rides in the snowy countryside. James Ives was hired to help draw pictures, and the two men

Nathaniel Currier and James Ives | *Winter Morning in the Country*, 1873
Currier & Ives, 125 Nassau Street, New York, Lithograph, handcolored, 8⅜ × 12⅜ in

were such a good team that Ives became a full partner. Drawings were printed carefully on good paper, each hand-colored one by one. Colorists worked in an assembly-line process, each artist coloring just one area of the whole picture. Americans could finally own art, many for the first time, thanks to the company of Currier & Ives, who produced over 7,000 prints!

Assembly-Line Coloring

Materials

3 or more friends
black marker
white drawing paper
colored pencils

photocopies of one black-and-white drawing created by a child (one copy for each person in the group)

Process

1. Decide what kind of scene everyone in the group would like to work on coloring. Then one child draws the simple, bold scene with black marker.
2. An adult can make photocopies of the picture using good white paper. It is best to use a quality paper that is thicker than regular copier paper.
3. The group will decide how each part of the picture will be colored. One person can completely color one drawing as a master example to follow.
4. Set up the assembly line for the final coloring. Each artist in the line will use just one color and for one part of the scene, passing it to the next person when complete. Color as many different editions or copies as desired. It would be nice to have one for each of the artists in the assembly line. If the assembly line works like Currier & Ives, every picture should end up looking nearly the same. Some artists may take longer than others, so work out a system that keeps things moving.
5. When all the coloring is done, hang all the assembly-line prints on the wall. Compare them to see if they look identical or nearly identical.

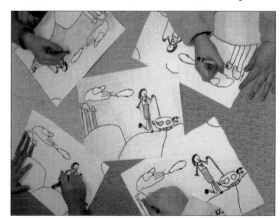

Five second graders create five identical Assembly-Line Coloring artworks from one original drawing created by Sydney, 8.

Louis Comfort Tiffany

Louis Comfort Tiffany | *Parrots Window*, c. 1905
Tiffany Studios, New York, leaded glass for the Watts-Sherman House in Newport, Rhode Island, Courtesy of the Charles Hosmer Morse Museum of American Art, Winter Park, Florida © Charles Hosmer Morse Foundation, Inc. 2008

February 18, 1848–January 17, 1933
Glass Artist, Art Nouveau

Louis Comfort Tiffany [TIF-uh-nee] grew up near New York City, where his family owned the famous Tiffany's jewelry store. As an adult, Tiffany created art with colored glass and sunshine. The windows he designed were made from thousands of tiny glass pieces, each color and type of glass specially made at Tiffany's factory. He made large windows for churches and public buildings, and smaller windows, lamps, and vases for private homes. Tiffany lampshades were especially popular because electric lights had just been invented, and people were enjoying the beauty of stained glass in their homes at night. Tiffany's work is part of the Art Nouveau style. His favorite subjects were flowers, plants, and people in natural settings.

Sometimes a beautiful work of art becomes part of everyday life, as with this little Tiffany *Parrots Window* book mark, available in the Museum Shop at the Charles Hosmer Morse Museum of American Art, Winter Park, Florida.

Bright Light Window Display

Stained glass is especially beautiful when light shines through and makes the colors glow. Because real glass is sharp and hard to cut, artists can instead create an easy light catcher with paints and a clear sheet of plastic that will look and shine like a Tiffany stained-glass window.

Materials

white glue, 4 oz.
  squeeze bottle
small jar with lid
choice of paint:
  watercolor,
  tempera, or
  acrylic

sheet of clear
  acrylic plastic
muffin tin, foam
  egg carton, or
  other small cups
paintbrush
water

Process

1. Squirt half of the white glue from the squeeze bottle into a small jar. Cover and save to use later in this project.

2. Add a few drops of black paint to the glue left in the squeeze bottle. Shake and stir until the glue turns gray. The gray glue will look like the metal lines that hold a stained-glass window together.

3. To make the design, you will squeeze the gray glue on the plastic sheet. You can create any abstract design, or you can sketch a design on paper first. Place the paper under the plastic and then follow the sketch with gray glue. The lines should connect with one another and go all around the outside, framing the design. The design can be in any shape: square, circle, oval, diamond, or custom.

4. Set the glue drawing on clear plastic aside to dry overnight. Once dry, place the plastic sheet over a sheet of white paper. Take out the jar of saved glue. Pour a bit of white glue into several cups of a muffin tin or a foam egg carton. Mix water into each cup of glue to make it thin and runny. Then add different colors of paint to each cup. Stir the paint into the glue with a paintbrush.

5. Paint the areas between the gray lines with colored glue. These areas become the "stained glass" of the Bright Light Window Display.

6. Let the window display dry overnight. Then use scissors to trim the outside edges of the plastic. Hang the window display in a widow so light shines through. The colors will come alive!

Tiffany Design Challenge

Tiffany used flowers for many of his designs. Find a photograph of a very large flower shown up close. Place it under a sheet of clear plastic. Use gray glue to trace its shapes and to frame it. Color the flower design with thin glue mixed with different colors of paint.

Let the Sun Shine In! Two Tiffany window works by Mrs. Van Slyke's second grade, Lynden, Washington

James McNeill Whistler

James McNeill Whistler | *Arrangement in Grey and Black: Portrait of the Painter's Mother*, 1871
Oil on canvas, 144.3 × 162.5 cm, Courtesy of Musée d'Orsay, Paris

July 11, 1834–July 17, 1903
Realist painter, Abstract

James McNeill Whistler [HWIS-lur] was one of the great characters of his era. He was flamboyant, egotistical, outspoken, and extremely talented. Whistler worked hard and painted wonderful works but was never associated with any particular style of art. His early portrait paintings were realistic, while later landscapes were nearly abstracts. He bridged traditions and did it with his own unique style. Whistler's painting titled *Arrangement in Grey and Black* (better known as *Whistler's Mother*) is one of the icons of American art. Yet Whistler left America as a young man and lived the rest of his life in Europe. Whistler was born in Massachusetts and spent a large part of his childhood in Russia, where his father worked building a railroad. In later years, he claimed to actually be from Russia, saying, "I shall be born when and where I wish." One story about Whistler's most famous painting, the portrait of his mother, Anna McNeill Whistler, tells that he wanted to paint her as a standing figure, but she was uncomfortable standing for so long and so brought in her own chair for the portrait session. Apparently Whistler went along with her wishes, and a great American painting was created. *Arrangement in Grey and Black* now resides in the Musée d'Orsay in Paris.

Side-View Portrait

Draw a mother's portrait from a side view. Choose to color or paint the drawing. Painting on watercolor paper instead of drawing paper is a special activity for artists interested in fine work. Watercolor paper is thicker than drawing paper, has a rough texture, and absorbs watercolor paint beautifully. It is inspiring to experience real watercolor paper now and then, and cutting an expensive sheet into smaller squares makes it economical. Watercolor paper also comes in tear-off pads.

Materials

a mom (or friend) to pose for the portrait
drawing paper or watercolor paper
pencil
coloring tools: crayons, colored pencils, or watercolor paints, brushes, and water

Process

❶ Invite Mom or any special person to pose for a portrait, just as Anna Whistler did for her artist son, James.

Mom can sit in a chair reading a book, sewing, snoozing, or watching TV. She will be sitting for a little while, so she should be comfortable. Ask Mom to hold a pose while being sketched.

❷ Choose to use drawing paper or watercolor paper. If using drawing paper, draw with pencil before coloring or painting. If using watercolor paper, sketch very lightly with pencil first. Draw Mom from the side, creating a full body profile portrait in the style of *Whistler's Mother*.

❸ Fill in the color on the drawing with crayons, colored pencils, or watercolor paints.

Klem's Mother, Side View, by Eric Klem, 12

John Singer Sargent

January 12, 1856–April 14, 1925
Realist painter, Portrait

John Singer Sargent [SAHR-juhnt] was a great American painter who never lived in the United States. His parents were Americans living in Europe, where he was born and lived his entire life. He traveled to the United States but always as a visitor. Sargent was a talented hard worker who painted constantly. He is best known for painting portraits and landscapes during his travels around the world. He painted famous people, world leaders, wealthy Americans, and businessmen. He also painted working people and poor street children with the same skill and attention that he gave to his wealthy clients. Although he worked during a time when other artists were exploring more abstract styles of art, Sargent was a firm Realist. He painted things exactly the way he saw them. The honesty of his work, combined with incredible skill in the thousands of paintings he created, make Sargent a truly great American artist.

Great Reproduction

The beautiful portraits of John Singer Sargent are perfect for a traditional art activity—drawing a reproduction of a great work of art. Art students often practice by copying famous paintings and sculptures. When you visit an art museum, you will often find artists with their sketchpads respectfully studying and copying great art. Fine artists copy or reproduce the paintings of other artists in order to practice new styles and techniques, skills they can then bring to their own original work. Any artist's work can be the subject of this activity: realistic paintings, abstracts, sculpture, and all other designs. Reproduce or practice copying a Sargent portrait with a choice of drawing materials.

Materials

drawing paper
pencils and eraser
choice of coloring tools: crayons, charcoal,
    colored chalk, oil pastels, pens, marking pens,
    colored pencils

Process

1. Select a portrait by Sargent from a library book or from the Internet. Look at it carefully, and then try to draw a picture of the painting. Work with any drawing tool in the list.
2. Draw lightly at first, sketching the shapes of the painting and noticing the choices Sargent made as he painted face, clothing, and background. Is the person shown from the front or turned to one side? Look at the rich textures of clothing and the patterns made by the dark and light shapes in the painting. Sargent paid close attention to every detail.
3. After sketching lightly, finish the drawing using one of the techniques listed here. (This is called a value study.)
   • Draw an exact copy of Sargent's painting.
   • Draw thick, smooth outlines of Sargent's painting, like a coloring-book picture.
   • Use pencils or chalks to fill in the tones of the Sargent painting, showing solid black areas, darkest areas, medium areas, and the lightest shades
   • Turn the Sargent painting upside down, and draw it again, upside down.

John Singer Sargent | *Mrs. Joshua Montgomery Sears*, 1899
Oil on canvas, (110 Kb); 147.6 × 96.8 cm (58⅛ × 38⅛ in), Museum of Fine Arts, Houston, Texas

Great Lady, by Irina Ammosova, 8

19

William Sidney Mount

William Sidney Mount | *Caught Napping (Boys Caught Napping in a Field)*, 1948
Oil on canvas, 29⅟₁₆ × 36⅛ in (73.8 × 91.7 cm), Dick S. Ramsay Fund, # 39.608, Brooklyn Museum, Brooklyn, New York

William Sidney Mount | *Dancing on the Barn Floor*, 1831
Oil on canvas, 25 × 31 in, Gift of Mr. and Mrs. Ward Melville, 1955, The Long Island Museum of American Art, History, and Carriages, Stony Brook, New York

November 26, 1807–November 19, 1868
Realist, Genre, Narrative

William Sidney Mount grew up on a farm on New York's Long Island. His older brother, who ran a sign-painting shop in New York City, encouraged him to paint. After studying art in college, Mount returned to the family farm at Setauket to begin his career, painting realistic portraits and local scenes. Because he was also a musician, many of his paintings feature music and dance. He traveled with a paint kit and his flute and fiddle, sketching pictures of his neighbors at work and play. Mount's paintings became very popular and appeared in books or prints. People appreciated that his paintings showed unique American themes of farm life, small towns, and portraits of common people. Other artists began to imitate Mount and paint similar subjects, but Mount's paintings are still considered to be the best images of life in America before the Civil War.

Real Painting

Adult supervision may be required

Mount painted pictures of the countryside and small towns of rural Long Island. His paint kit contained all the things he needed to sketch scenes and paint complete pictures on location. Put together a traveling paint kit and head outdoors to paint a real scene with watercolors. Because there's less control, painting on location allows young artists to be loose and spontaneous and to share their love of art with friends and neighbors.

Apple Tree, by Ivan A. Smith-Garcia, 6

Materials

watercolor paint set with mixing tray
paintbrushes
plastic bottle of water
container to rinse brushes, rag
pad of watercolor paper or sheets of paper taped onto a small board
pencil, permanent marker
tote bag, backpack, or old purse

Process

1 Assemble a traveling painting kit containing the painting supplies mentioned in the materials list. Go for a walk around the neighborhood to locate a scene for a painting, or head to a city park, playground, beach, public garden, or favorite backyard. If you are leaving your own yard, adult permission and supervision are required.

2 Find a safe place to sit and create a painting like a picnic table, park bench, or blanket on the lawn. Set up the art materials, pouring water into the rinse container.

3 Sketch the scene with pencil. This could be as large as a panorama of the landscape or as detailed as a close-up of a flower or a fire hydrant. Some artists like to use only light pencil strokes to define the main shapes and areas of a painting, while other artists prefer drawing a complete picture with pencil or pen before starting to paint.

4 Dip a brush into water, wet the watercolor paints, and start painting. Mix paints together to create colors seen in real objects. Let the paintbrush sweep across the paper. Use plenty of water. Be bold and carefree, and paint happily!

2

New American Ideas

Anne-Sophie Furlong

Chloe Crookall

Max Currer

Caroline Fairbank

Alexandra Fernandez-Hassel

Eliza Fischer

Katherine Apushkin

Ariana Moulton's 2008 third grade class from Lincoln Elementary, Chicago, Illinois, shares several of their works interpreting Grant Wood's iconic painting, *American Gothic* (see Grant Wood, p. 52).

Edward Hopper

Edward Hopper | *Chop Suey*, 1929
Oil on canvas, Courtesy of Barney A. Ebsworth, private collection

July 22, 1882–May 15, 1967
Realist painter

Edward Hopper [HOP-er] was a Realist who painted pictures of America during the first half of the 1900s. While many artists of his time were exploring abstract art and pure design, Hopper chose to paint scenes of real American life—everyday, ordinary scenes that became very powerful with Hopper's vision. Hopper grew up in the Hudson River town of Nyack, New York. He loved the boats along the river and once wanted to be a shipbuilder but decided on a career as an artist. In 1900, he moved to New York City to study art and to become a professional illustrator and painter. For a period of time, he was part of the group of artists who called themselves the Ashcan School (see George Bellows, p. 30). He lived in Paris for several years, and then he returned to New York where he lived and worked the rest of his life. Hopper is best known for artwork that portrays a feeling of loneliness. His paintings often picture an open window in the corner of an empty room, a lone person sitting by a window, or several people together yet lost in thought and separated from each other. His landscapes show isolated houses in the country or bleak city streets. Yet Hopper's paintings are rich with simple shapes and colors and glowing light. His unique style and the emotional power of his paintings make Edward Hopper a true American artistic genius.

Feelings Wash Over

Edward Hopper's paintings express emotions like loneliness, happiness, anger, joy, or sadness. When the drawing is complete, wash over it with thinned tempera paint in a color to express that emotion.

Materials

crayons, colored pencils, or permanent markers
marking pens (optional: water-based markers blur and bleed when wet, a unique effect)
white drawing paper
masking tape
"emotion" color tempera paint, thinned with water
watercolor paints
soft paintbrush
paper towel, tissue, rag, or clean sponge

Process

❶ Think of an emotion to express through drawing. Facial expressions are a good beginning way to draw emotional expression. Smiling, crying, frowning, and smirking are examples. Other ideas to draw that express emotion are: friends at a party, view of a cemetery, snowy night, rainbows, holiday event, colors and shapes, lost pet, lines and designs, looking out a window, clouds and sky.

❷ Draw and color the picture on white paper. Any style of drawing will do, whether fully detailed or simple and bold.

❸ When the drawing is complete, tape all four sides to the table or workspace with masking tape lightly pressed to the paper.

❹ Think about what color paint-wash will express the emotion of the drawing. Mix a little paint in a container of clear water. The water should have color, but only enough to color the paper lightly.

❺ Wash over the drawing with the thinned paint, using a soft brush that holds a generous amount of the wash. Cover the entire drawing with thin color. Extra puddles may be soaked away with paper towels, tissue, or a clean sponge. Then let dry.

❻ Carefully peel the masking tape from the paper. A clean, unpainted frame will remain.

Relaxed and Content, by Sydney P., 8

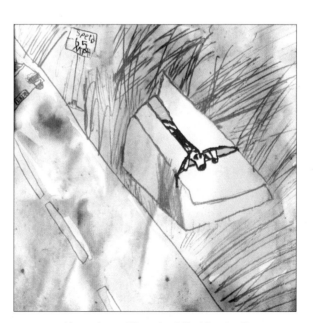

Abandoned Pup, by Nile Kirwin, 9

Scared Bear, by Cameron Bol, 8

Frank Lloyd Wright

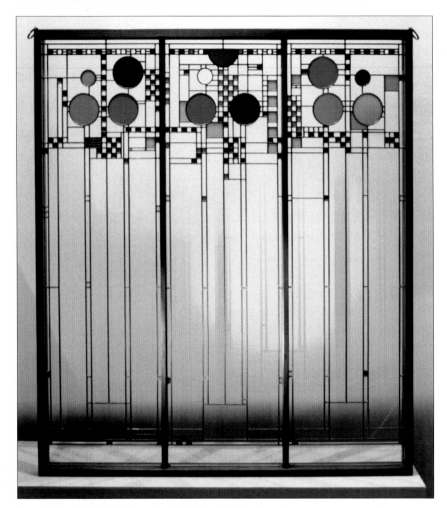

June 8, 1867–April 9, 1959
Architect, Glass artist

Frank Lloyd Wright [rite] was born in a small town in Wisconsin. As a boy, one of his favorite toys was a set of wooden blocks. Block houses and imaginary cities were his first architectural designs! Wright became America's most famous architect. He designed houses, churches, skyscrapers, resorts, museums, and bridges. Many people don't know he also designed stained-glass windows, furniture, and other decorations for the inside of his buildings. In fact, some of Wright's art deco windows are the most beautiful ever designed. He used simple geometric shapes in the buildings and patterns he invented. Frank Lloyd Wright's buildings and other designs can be seen all over the world. Some of his best stained-glass windows are in a little school he designed called the Avery Coonley Playhouse. His work created a style of architecture and window design that is uniquely American.

Frank Lloyd Wright | *Coonley Playhouse Triptych*
Art glass, 3 panels, 24 × 81 in, Avery Coonley House, Riverside, Illinois, 1911 | Courtesy Oakbrook-Esser Studios. All Rights Reserved.

Frank Lloyd Wright | Avery Coonley House
300 Scottswood Road/281 Bloomingbank Road, Riverside, Cook County
Plate #117 TERRACE FRONT HABS, ILL,16-RIVSI,2-4, Library of Congress, © 2008
Frank Lloyd Wright Foundation / Artists Rights Society (ARS), New York

Bubble Window

Frank Lloyd Wright designed cheerful windows with bubbles and other geometric shapes for the children's Coonley Playhouse. One even has a tiny American flag peeking between squares and lines. Create a bubble window by cutting art tissue and sticking it to large pieces of clear adhesive contact paper in a preplanned pattern. Then sandwich the shapes with a second sheet of contact paper. Last, trace shapes with a permanent black marker, or draw lines with black marker to represent the window partitions. Display in a window and let the sun shine in!

Materials

clear contact paper (roll of
  adhesive vinyl, clear)
scissors
bright colors of art tissue
objects with shapes to trace,
  different sizes
circles: quarter, half dollar,
  cup, bowl

squares and rectangles: small
  box, post-it note, product
  box, piece of cardboard
pen for tracing
permanent marking pen
ruler, yardstick, or straight
  edge
optional: black masking tape

Process

1. Consider how wide or tall to make the window. Start with one width of contact paper about 24-inches long. Then add more to make the window bigger, taller, or wider as desired. To make the window larger, simply stick and join contact paper segments together. Set aside.
2. Choose colors of art tissue. Trace shapes of selected objects on the tissue. Then cut out the shapes.
3. Lay the pieces of colored tissue on the work table in a pattern.
4. Place the peeled and sticky contact paper next to the pieces. Begin pressing the pieces into place. Feel free to change the pattern. Cut more pieces as needed, and press into place.
5. When all the pieces are final, an adult can help add the top layer of contact paper to the artwork. Peel the panel and hold the contact paper over the artwork. Begin pressing this top piece at the corners, and press until the entire artwork is covered. Expect bubbles and some wrinkles, which can be pressed out fairly well. Trim away any extra contact paper edges.
6. Rub the entire artwork with a straight edge to make it shinier. The back of a spoon works very well. Rub and rub!
7. To make the work look like stained glass, add black lines by tracing around the shapes with a permanent marker. Long lines can be drawn with a yardstick. Add a black line around the outside edge like a frame. (If black masking tape is available, pull a long piece the entire length of the edge of the window art to create a frame.)
8. Tape in a sunny window to enjoy.

Group Idea: Several different window panes from numerous artists can be joined together with tape to make one huge bubble window!

Wild Window, by Cody, 8

Three Panel Bubble Window, by classmates Maddison Fox, McKenzie Thompson, and Tori Crabtree, 8

Gutzon Borglum

Photograph of Mount Rushmore
courtesy of Dean Franklin, 2003

March 25, 1867–March 6, 1941
Realist sculptor

Gutzon Borglum [BOR-gluhm], the great American sculptor, carved the monument of giant faces of four great American presidents in the side of Mount Rushmore, a great granite mountain. Gutzon Borglum was born in Idaho and grew up in the western states. He studied art in France and returned to the United States to work as a sculptor. Museums bought his works, and soon he had a fine national reputation. He was invited to create a monumental work at Mount Rushmore in South Dakota. Borglum decided to carve four popular presidents. He sculpted giant clay models and hiked over the mountainside to pick the best placement for each face. Work began on the stone cliffs in 1927. For 14 years, crews of workmen carefully blasted away chunks of rock and carved the cliff face with huge tools under Borglum's direction. The carving ended when Borglum died in 1941. The giant faces became a national park that is visited by thousands of people every day of every year.

Carved Clay

With a homemade wire-loop carving tool, carve a small-scale sculpture in a block of soft clay.

Materials

1-2 pounds of clay	2 or 3 paperclips
6-inch square of heavy cardboard or wood	2 or 3 clothespins masking tape

Process

1. Make 2 or 3 wire-loop tools to use for the clay carving. Bend a paperclip by hand into a rounded or pointed shape, then pinch the wire ends with a clothespin. Wrap the clothespin tightly with masking tape or duct tape to secure the wire and create a handle.

2. Choose a subject for the carved clay statue. Sculpting a face in the style of Mount Rushmore is one possibility. Animals make excellent subjects, especially animals sitting, lying down, or curled into compact forms. (Hint: Avoid figures with slender parts like legs or outstretched arms.) Abstract sculptures are always interesting, and any sculpture can develop into an abstract if realism proves frustrating.

3. Press and shape the soft clay into a rough shape set firmly on a cardboard or wooden base. Gently carve away bits of clay with the wire-loop tools, pulling the wire slowly through the clay to remove a little bit at a time. Avoid the temptation to mold the clay with fingers. Carving is a completely different way to create a sculpture.

4. As the clay is removed, imagine a stone sculptor working with hammers and chisels, or workmen high on the face of a cliff setting dynamite charges for each bit of rock removed in the carving of Mount Rushmore. Once clay is removed, don't put it back, even though the soft clay would allow this.

5. When the clay sculpture is finished, follow the directions for the type of clay used to let it dry and harden or remain soft.

Photograph by
Morgan Van Slyke

Landon VanBerkum, 8,
carves a clay face.
Photograph © Rebecca
Van Slyke 2008

Grandma Moses

September 7, 1860–December 13, 1961
Folk Art painter

Grandma Moses [MOH-zis] took up painting when she was in her 70s and painted 1,600 paintings, more than 225 of them after her 100th birthday! She lived until she was 101. Grandma Moses began her life a year before the Civil War as Anna Mary Robertson, the third of 10 children, and was warmly encouraged by her father to draw and paint. She later met and married Thomas Moses, and together they farmed with their five surviving children. Years later, after Thomas Moses died, Anna Mary Moses, known then as Grandma Moses to everyone, began painting scenes of life and celebrations seen in upstate New York where she had lived most of her life. Grandma Moses was a self-taught painter. She painted from the sky down: first the sky, then the mountains, next the land, and last of all, the tiny busy people. She worked from memory on pieces of pressed wood painted white or on strong cardboard. Grandma Moses was feisty, strong, kind, and one of the most famous folk artists in 20th century America. Grandma Moses once said, "Painting's not important. . . .The important thing is keeping busy. If I didn't start painting, I would have raised chickens."

Grandma Moses | *Apple Butter Making*, 1953
(K 653) Copyright © March 1953, (renewed February 1981),
Grandma Moses Properties Co., New York

Busy Season

Portray a scene, real or imaginary, in a neighborhood, classroom, playground, park, or other busy location. Paint it to take place in summer, fall, winter, or spring. Add busy people and all the details of their busy lives, celebrations, or activities characterized by the time of the year.

Materials

white material to paint on: flat piece of wood painted white, cardboard painted white, heavy white paper, cardboard covered with white paper, white posterboard, white cardboard box lid
tempera or acrylic paints
paintbrushes in various sizes, including small and fine-point
container of water, rag
colored pencils and fine-point permanent markers (optional)

Process

❶ Think of a busy scene that would be interesting to imagine or remember. Think of the time of year of that scene. Choosing to paint an imaginary or pretend scene is fine to do.

❷ Begin by preparing the background of the scene to go with a season. Summer will have bright light and warm colors; winter will have blues and whites; spring will have greens and yellows; and fall will have warmer shades of color. Paint from the sky down like Grandma Moses, making mountains or hills with a larger brush and paint. Let dry.

❸ Next, add as many activities and people, characters, pets, houses, and so on as desired. Fill the scene with activities and details. Use paint and a small brush. If preferred, fine or medium-tip permanent markers will also work well on the painted background if it is completely dry.

❹ When everything feels right, the painting is ready to dry.

Hans Hofmann

Hans Hofmann | *Combinable Wall I and II*, 1961
Oil on canvas, 112½ × 84½ in, Berkeley Art Museum/Pacific Film Archive, Gift of Hans Hofmann,
1963.10, Courtesy of Renata, Hans, and Maria Hofmann Trust / Artists Rights Society (ARS), New York

March 21, 1880–February 17, 1966
Abstract Expressionist painter

Hans Hofmann [HOF-muhn] is called an Abstract Expressionist as well as a Fauvist and a Cubist; he is all of these, and he also created his own new style of powerful and unique paintings known for their energetic clashing colors and design. Hofmann was born in Germany and grew up in Munich. He studied architecture before he began to paint. When he moved to the United States, he became known as the most important and influential American artist in this country and as the leader of Abstract Expressionism in America. Hofmann was a renowned inspirational art teacher with his own art schools and was recognized for helping students develop their individual ways of creating art. Hofmann encouraged his students to visit museums and art galleries so they could see many kinds of art. Many of Hofmann's students became famous artists (see Wolf Kahn, p.62). Hans Hofmann once said, "Art is essential to being fully human."

Energetic Color Blocks

Hofmann's signature style often shows bold color blocks layered with an energetic painted surface and overlapping shapes. With no particular preplanned design, paint with bright colors to create shapes that fill the paper as they overlap and join. Blocks and rectangles of art tissue can be pressed into the paint to highlight the design.

Materials

tempera paints in bright
  colors
paintbrushes

large sheet of drawing paper
art tissue in bright colors
scissors

Process

❶ To begin, paint the entire sheet of drawing paper with two or more large areas of color (rectangles or other large shapes). Then dry.

❷ With a free hand, paint large blocks of color on the painted drawing paper, making them overlap. Rectangles and squares will be most like Hofmann's work, but any shapes are expressive.

❸ Allow the painting to dry or proceed to the Art Tissue steps to add colored shapes to the painting.

Lots of Color Blocks, by
Brianna George, 5

Art Tissue Press-In

While the painted shapes are still wet, tear or cut matching shapes from art tissue and press each shape into the paint shape. Allow the shapes of tissue to overlap. No glue is needed. Dry the entire artwork completely.

Charles Demuth

November 8, 1883–October 23, 1935
American Precisionist, Modernist

Most of Charles Demuth's [DEE-mith] work was painted in his hometown of Lancaster, Pennsylvania, which gave him his subject matter—acrobats, cafés, vaudeville, and his mother's flower garden at home, which Demuth could view from his upstairs bedroom studio. From an early age, Demuth was frail and ill and walked with a cane. When he died at age 52, he left behind over a thousand works of art, some bold, some delicate. Though Demuth's beach scene watercolors painted at Cape Cod are his best works, most agree that Demuth is best known for a painting called *Number 5 in Gold*. This painting is a unique portrait of Demuth's friend, William Carlos Williams, who wrote the poem "The Great Figure." The poem describes the experience of seeing a red fire engine with the number five painted on it, racing through city streets. Demuth's portrait consists not of a likeness of his friend but instead is a grouping of images that remind the artist of his friend—the poet's initials WCW and the names "Bill" and "Carlos" are intermixed with images from the fire engine poem.

Charles Demuth | *I Saw the Figure Five in Gold*, 1928
Oil on board, 35 × 30 in, Metropolitan Museum of Art, New York,
Permission from Demuth Museum, Lancaster, PA

Homage Portrait Collage

Create an artwork that features images associated with a good friend's interests and life, yet is not a portrait of how the friend actually looks. Use basic materials like colored markers and magazine cut-outs on white drawing paper. For a bright touch, highlight an important aspect of the work with gold paint.

Materials

pencil
magazine
   clippings
large white
   drawing paper
scissors

colored markers,
   wide and fine tip
glue
gold paint and
   small brush
a friend to honor

Process

1. Think of a good friend or family member. Think of images that relate to that person, such as things this person likes or enjoys doing. Some ideas are:

   Sports: soccer, basketball, skateboarding
   Pets: cat, dog, fish, snake, gerbil
   Food: dessert, sandwich, spaghetti
   Fashion: hat, shoes, jewelry

   Friendship: overnights, birthdays, playing
   Hobbies: reading, fishing, painting, horses
   Family: car, bike, house, apartment
   Interests: travel, books, dreams

2. With a pencil, begin lightly drawing images from this special person's life on the drawing paper. Begin with one idea and add more to fill the paper in a collage fashion. Color and outline the images with colored markers. Some areas can be left white or uncolored, too.

3. Include the person's name, initials, or parts of the name within the artwork.

4. Add magazine clippings with glue to further represent the person's life and interests.

5. Choose to paint one important, main image in the portrait homage with gold paint to show how important it is in this person's life. For example, if this person loves playing soccer more than anything in the world, paint the soccer image with gold paint. If this person enjoys baking fancy desserts, paint the dessert image with gold paint. Let the painting collage dry well.

6. Show the portrait to the special person being honored. Can they guess who is featured in the artwork?

Happy Thirteenth Birthday!, by Julia Kim, 11

29

George Bellows

George Bellows | *The Circus*, 1912
Oil on canvas, 33⅞ × 43⅞ in, Gift of Elizabeth Paine Metcalf, 1947.8,
Addison Gallery of American Art, Phillips Academy, Andover, Massachusetts

August 12 or 19, 1882–
January 8, 1925
Realist painter, Ashcan School

George Bellows [BEL-ohz] came to New York from Ohio, where he was a college athlete and sports hero. Everyone expected him to play baseball, but he worked to become an artist instead. Bellows is the best-known painter of the Ashcan School, a group of artists living in New York City in the early 1900s who often painted pictures of people living in crowded city neighborhoods. Critics named this style "ashcan" to mock the artists who chose common subjects instead of more traditional ideas. The Ashcan artists and their bold, powerful paintings paved the way for art to make social change and a better world. Bellows's best-known paintings are of prize fighting, a sport that was outlawed in his time. His rough brushstrokes show men struggling at the limits of their strength, lit dramatically in the dark atmosphere of the boxing ring. Bellows gained his fame as a young man, and while he enjoyed being part of the rebellious Ashcan group, he also painted portraits of wealthy patrons, landscapes of New England, and beautiful pictures of his young daughters. *The Circus* is a perfect example of Ashcan School art by George Bellows.

Sports Figures

Materials

photographs of an athlete in action, from sports magazines or from the Internet
8½ × 11-inch heavy white drawing paper
pencil and eraser

colored marker pens
examples of baseball cards or other sports cards, if available

Process

❶ Choose a favorite athlete to draw—someone who plays base-ball, football, basketball, or soccer, a swim champion, gymnast, ballet dancer, figure skater, or even a boxer. Locate a photo of the athlete in action. Sports magazines are a good source, but a quick search of the athlete's name on the Internet leads to a large selection of photos that can be printed as a model for a drawing.

❷ Look at the photo. Draw a similar athlete, filling the paper. Sketch with a pencil, then outline the figure with bold marker lines. Finish the drawing with bold colors.

❸ Drawn athlete forms may be cut out and pasted on a solid background of mat board or construction paper, or the drawing may be finished by coloring in the background.

Soccer Man, by Beau-Jean Martin, 5

Sports Card

❶ Create a Sports Card by compiling details about the athlete on the reverse side of the drawing. Include the athlete's name and birth date.

❷ Add any other facts or sports achievements. Include a drawing of the team logo, if it is appropriate.

Some ideas to include:

team	position	records	achievements
photo	nationality	career years	

❸ Make additional cards and organize in them a box, folder, or notebook. Friends can trade cards with each other!

Gymnast, by Kristi Busse, 9

Joseph Cornell

Joseph Cornell | *Soap Bubble Set*, 1936
Mixed media, 15¾4 × 14¼ in, Wadsworth Atheneum Museum of Art, Hartford, Connecticut. Purchased through the gift of Henry and Walter Keney, 1928.270, Art © The Joseph and Robert Cornell Memorial Foundation/Licensed by VAGA, New York, NY

December 24, 1903–December 29, 1972
Surrealist assemblage sculptor

Joseph Cornell [kor-NEL] was born the day before Christmas in Nyack, New York. He grew up in Queens with his mother and his brother, Robert. Here he remained and lived, caring for Robert, who had cerebral palsy, while creating his art, collecting, sorting, and grouping his collections, memorabilia, relics, and bits of treasure. He is best known for his boxes constructed with assemblages of objects and trinkets, maps and photographs, engravings and drawings, bric-a-brac and ornaments. Cornell, a completely self-taught artist, is one of the originators of the form of sculpture called assemblage, where unlikely objects are joined together in an intriguing unity. He spent most of his time working alone on his boxes, leaving his home to search for things that would become part of his personal assemblages, scavenging in New York junk shops and flea markets for whatever caught his imagination and satisfied his creativity. To Cornell, his assemblages were treasures of memories and dreams, an assortment of things waiting for his creative energy to place them in groupings of highly personal meaning. His studio was a place for sorting, filing, and mixing his objects with his own mementos and eventually working them into his art. From all this, he made his boxes, some taking many years to complete. Some are playful, some sad and lonely, others express love and devotion, and still others are curiously designed to make people pause and think. Cornell's boxes were not created to share with admirers or collectors of art; they were made as gifts for people living or long dead who had touched his life in some way known to him alone.

Box Assemblage

Materials

a box: cardboard school-supply box, shoe box, fancy chocolates box, box with see-through lid, jewelry box, pizza box, small fruit crate, stationery box, compartmentalized box
paper to cover the box and to decorate or give meaning to the assemblage: magazine or catalog pictures, colorful tissue, wrapping paper, foil paper, old greeting cards or postcards, maps, travel brochures, newspaper comics, old torn books, photocopies, printed pages, sheet music

collection of found objects (let the theme guide selection): beads or pieces of old jewelry, small toys, parts of toys, party favors, trinkets, mementos, toy figures or animals, small objects, decorations, ornaments, wire, leaves, twigs, shells, rocks, craft items, fabric, sewing trim, machine parts, miniatures

drawing or painting materials: gold or silver pens, acrylic paint, markers or pens, colored pencils, crayons, chalk, pastels, liquid watercolor paints, glitter glue, pencil

materials for gluing or adhering: white glue, glue stick, tape, hobby coating, glue gun, stapler

brushes

clear plastic wrap

scissors

Process

❶ Choose a theme to guide the artwork. The box can illustrate a special time or place, like a trip to the beach or a walk on a winter day. It might show a favorite activity, like skateboarding or riding horses. It could express a feeling, a dream, or a memory.

❷ Cover the inside of the box with decorative paper to fit the theme. To do this, lay the box on top of a sheet of paper. Then trace the edges with a pencil, cut the paper a bit smaller than the traced lines, and glue the cut paper into the box. Cover the sides of the box in the same way, both inside and out.

❸ Choose the objects or materials that will go into the box, again keeping the theme in mind. Spread this collection out on the table beside the box. Then arrange and fit the items into the box. Look at Cornell's boxes to see how his materials are stacked, attached, and placed into the box space.

❹ The box will stand upright when the artwork is finished, so things must be glued in place. Think of ways to create spaces within a box. You can:
- divide the box into compartments with strips of cardboard
- use smaller boxes to make shelves and platforms
- stack things on top of each other
- hang things from the top of the box
- attach a stick across the box and hang things from it
- glue objects to the back, sides, or edges of the box

❺ When all the materials are assembled and glued down, a final sheet of clear plastic can be stretched over the front of the box to protect the delicate work, creating a "framed picture." Each box can be displayed upright, or a simple loop of string can be attached to the back to hang the box on the wall like a picture.

My Family Origin in Shelves: England, Germany, Scotland, by Hannah Kohl

Curious Party Box, by Francesca Martinelli, 6

Maria Martínez

Maria Martínez, San Ildefonso Pueblo
Photograph courtesy of Jarrod Da', 2008

1884– July 20, 1980
Potter, Traditional native

Maria Martínez [mahr-TEEN-ehz], of San Ildefonso Pueblo near Santa Fe, New Mexico, is considered the most famous of all Native American potters for her treasured black-on-black pottery technique. For nearly 100 years, Martínez lived in the pueblo. Her passion for pottery-making began when she was a child, and her intense interest kept the pottery of the pueblo alive, even when pottery was not being used as much by her people. She and her husband, Julian, rediscovered the way to make the unique black-on-black pottery from pueblo clay and volcanic ash. They worked as a team while raising their family. Their children learned the pottery craft and helped in many ways. Her son, Popovi Da' [day], and her grandson, Tony Da', contributed major innovations in pottery-making and design. Tony's son and Maria's great-grandson, Jarrod Da', continues the family legacy through his native connected paintings. Just before Martínez died, she said, "When I am gone, essentially other people have my pots. But to you and the rest of my family, I leave my greatest achievement, the ability to make the pottery."

Coil Pottery

One of the oldest ways of making pottery is with coils. Long "snakes" or coils of clay are laid next to each other, then blended together by smoothing the coils flat. In this project, coils are placed in a soup bowl, which acts as a mold and helps create the final bowl shape.

Materials

small bowl (soup or breakfast cereal size)
plastic wrap
air-drying terra cotta clay or other clay
acrylic paints and brushes

Process

Photograph by Kim Solga

1. Line the bowl with plastic wrap.
2. Soften the clay by squeezing and kneading. Pinch off balls of clay the size of a plum or walnut. Roll these balls into long snakes.
3. Place one end of a clay snake in the bottom of the bowl. Coil the clay around itself, making a round clay spiral. Add a second clay snake next to the first coil. Coil it in a different direction, or form it into two spirals creating a fancy S shape. Keep adding clay snakes and coiling them against the others until the bowl is filled, completely lined with clay coils up to the edge.
4. Gently smooth the inside of the clay with fingertips. Push hard enough to blend the coils together.
5. Let the clay dry for a day or two, until the clay is completely hard.
6. Tip the coil bowl out of the soup bowl. Peel away the plastic wrap. The pattern of the coils makes a design on the outside of the clay. If the inner surface of the coil bowl is still soft, let it dry for another day.
7. Paint the dry clay bowl with acrylic paints. Display the finished bowl as a piece of art, great for holding small objects such as coins, office supplies, or potpourri.

Elijah Pierce

March 5, 1892–May 7, 1984
Folk Art sculptor, Wood Carver

Elijah Pierce [peers], the youngest son of formerly enslaved parents, was born on a farm in Mississippi. Here he began carving as a child with a treasured pocketknife that his father gave him. By age seven, Pierce was carving little wooden farm animals that he gave away to friends at school. From earliest childhood, Pierce was encouraged to believe God had called him to preach through his wood carvings, which tell stories. His carvings depict African American sports heroes, Bible stories, and political topics, but he is best known for his religious carvings including the *Book of Wood*, a series of 33 large reliefs. Pierce was also a barber, and his barbershop on Long Street in Columbus, Ohio, was a favorite place for men to gather and talk over the news of the world and for Pierce to preach. It wasn't until the early 1970s that Pierce's carvings became known outside his small community. Many people in the art world have written about the tremendous influence Pierce had with his art, but it's the people who knew him personally that tell us Pierce was a kind and gentle person and a friend to many, as well as a great artist. The Martin Luther King Jr. Performing and Cultural Arts Complex named the Elijah Pierce Gallery in his honor, and the Columbus Museum of Art owns over 300 of Pierce's carvings.

Elijah Pierce | *The Book of Wood*, 1936
Carved and painted wood relief, Columbus Museum of Art, Ohio, Museum Purchase 1985.003.002a-d

Bas Relief Clay Carving

Materials

clay
cookie sheet with edges
paper, pencil
choice of tools for carving, etching, and digging clay:
    plastic knife, toothpick, popsicle stick, melon baller, paper clip, cuticle stick, bamboo skewer, screwdriver, straight edge, clay tools

Sammie VanLoo, 8, carves a green fish bas relief.

Process

1. Spread and press clay by hand 1- to 2- inches thick over the entire surface of a cookie sheet with sides or a baking pan (use real clay or Plasticine). Uniformly spread clay with a spatula or straight edge to flatten and smooth.
2. Think of a very simple design or picture for the bas relief work. Draw it on paper. Use few details. Bold, simple lines work best. With a toothpick or bamboo skewer, draw the same design, large and bold, on the clay surface. It's easy to change or erase using a finger to smudge away marks. Draw a frame, if desired, around the edge of the clay.
3. With a carving or digging tool, begin to remove the clay from around the design, so the design stands up and the rest of the clay is low and cut away. The frame will also be raised, although it can have designs cut into it for decoration. Add other detail like dots or lines.
4. If using real clay, the work can dry until hard. Display it in the pan—it's difficult to remove it in one piece, though worth a try. If using Plasticine, it will remain soft.

Horace Pippin

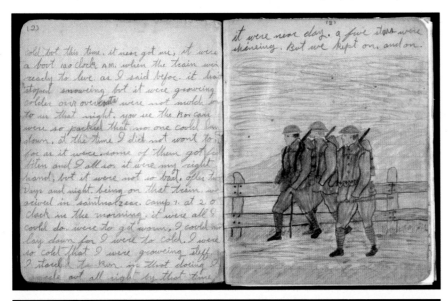

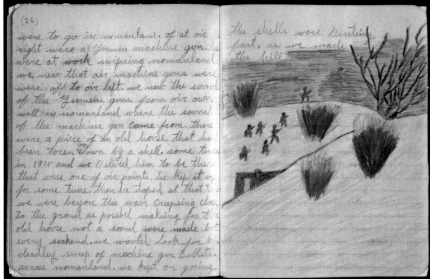

Horace Pippin's Autobiography, First World War, 192-
Horace Pippin, journal: 62 p.: handwritten; 22 × 18 cm. Courtesy of the Horace Pippin papers, circa 1920s, 1943, Archives of American Art, Smithsonian Institution.

February 22, 1888–July 6, 1946
Folk painter, Illustrator

Horace Pippin [PIP-in], a self-taught African American painter, was born in West Chester, Pennsylvania, just 23 years after the end of slavery. His grandparents were slaves, and his parents were domestic workers. At the age of three, Pippin and his family moved to Goshen, New York, where he went to school in a one-room segregated school. Pippin liked to draw and would illustrate his spelling words in school. But his family could not afford art materials for their talented son. At age 10, he won a box of crayons in a magazine drawing contest and started coloring. When Pippin was an adult, he fought in World War I as a member of the 369th Army Regiment, the first African American soldiers to fight overseas for the United States. During the war, he kept a diary in a notebook with drawings and descriptions of battles and his days overseas. His diary is a day-by-day account of what war is like and how it made him feel. Pippin was seriously wounded in his right arm, but when he came home from the war, he found a way to paint again. First he made burnt-wood art panels by drawing on wood using a hot poker. Then Pippin decided to try painting with oil. He used his "good" left hand to guide his injured right hand, which held the paintbrush across the canvas. It took him three years to finish his first painting. He said, "The pictures come to me in my mind and if to me it is a worthwhile picture I paint it. I do over the picture several times in my mind and when I am ready to paint it I have all the details I need." He also painted historical subjects like Abraham Lincoln, scenes from the Bible, memories of war, and scenes from his childhood. He made 75 paintings during the last years of his life.

Daily Picture Diary

In a spiral-bound notebook with lined white pages, keep a diary with sketches and drawings of your daily activities for a week or more. Draw one page per day with colored pencils like Horace Pippin did. Add written captions and stories to go with the drawings.

Materials

spiral bound notebook (white pages with blue lines work well)
permanent marker
colored pencils or crayons
pencil with eraser

Process

❶ Label the front of the spiral notebook with a permanent marker. Name it something that describes what is inside, such as My Week at School, My Life, The Days of Becky, Private Diary of Mike, Picture Diary by Kim Jones, and so on.

❷ Open the notebook to an empty page to begin. Write the month, day, and year in a corner of the page to document the day of the drawing.

❸ Draw something that happened this first day of the picture diary. Sketch in pencil and color in with colored pencils. Crayons could also be used. Some ideas are:

fun activity by myself	family fun or trouble
memorable experience	dream last night
fun times with a friend	wishing my day could be
interesting experience at	this way
school	imaginary day

❹ Add comments, thoughts, feelings, or other descriptive words on the page.

❺ Set aside until the following day, and then begin again on a new page.

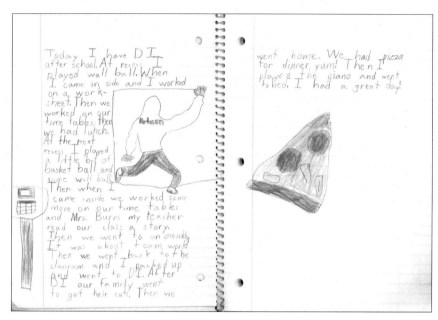

Daily Picture Diary, Destination Imagination Day,
by Alexander Petersen, 9

❻ Repeat the process of recording activities, thoughts, and feelings in the diary for at least seven days. Continue longer if desired.

❼ Decide if the picture diary is private or is to be shared. Then decide where to keep it. Some picture diary artists keep their diaries with them all the time.

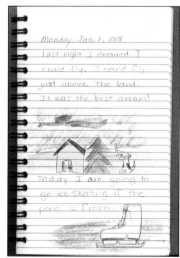

Daily Picture Diary, My Flying Dream,
by Ella Zahn, 9

Thomas Hart Benton

Thomas Hart Benton | *Independence*, 1961
Courtesy of the Truman Library, Independence, Missouri.
© Thomas Hart Benton and Rita P. Benton Testamentary
Trusts/UMB Bank Trustee. Licensed by VAGA, New York, NY

April 15, 1889–January 19, 1975
Regionalist painter

Thomas Hart Benton [BEN-tun] was a famous Regionalist painter whose style featured the rolling hills and farmlands of Missouri, the great Missouri River, and the magnificent Rocky Mountains. He is best known for his strong, colorful, larger-than-life paintings of landscapes, farmlands, and strong, lanky people at work. Benton was born in a small Ozark Mountain town and raised in Missouri. The wide-open spaces of the Midwest inspired his work throughout his life. His father first sent him to military school but eventually agreed to let him study art in Chicago and then in Europe. Benton believed there should be a uniquely American style of art, and he moved his family from New York City to Missouri when he was 35. It was then that his paintings began to focus on Americana. Through the Depression years of the 1930s, Benton painted many large murals that showed the power, dignity, and heroism of the common man. He developed a true American style that was different from any other artist in the world. Thomas Hart Benton's artwork showed his own special view of the American spirit.

Hero Mural

Many of Thomas Hart Benton's works were murals, very large paintings made to cover an entire wall. Some murals are painted right on the wall; others are painted on panels that fit the wall. Paint a mural to fit a door featuring a life-size Thomas Hart Benton hero!

Materials

large paper from a roll, as wide as a door
a helper
black marker, pen, or crayon
tempera paints
paintbrushes or sponge brushes, 1 inch wide
smaller paintbrushes for detail work
masking tape

Process

1. Roll out enough paper to cover one side of a door. An adult with a tape measure can help make the paper the right size.

2. Lie down on top of this big sheet of paper and place your arms and legs in an active pose. Pretend to be climbing a mountain, leaping up to catch a ball, dancing in a ballet, or speaking in front of a huge audience. Freeze in this pose on the paper. An adult helper or friend can trace all the way around your body with a marker or crayon. Then, carefully stand and see the tracing. There will be a life-size outline of the artist as a hero.

3. Use the marker to draw in the rest of the hero's clothing and other details. Draw clothes that match the hero's style. Draw the face and add details of the fingers of the hands. Finally, draw the background that makes the setting for the hero.

4. Use the large paintbrushes to paint the biggest areas of the mural first. Water down or thin the paint so it's not too thick; it should cover the paper easily. Use smaller paintbrushes to fill in areas where the wide brushes are too big. Finally, paint the hero. Painting everything might take several days to finish. Benton sometimes worked on his murals for months before they were done.

5. After the paint is dry, go back to outline things and draw details with the black marker.

6. With help, tape the finished mural to a door, closet door, or to a suitable wall.

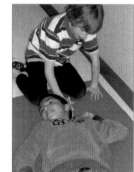

Isaac Dykstra, 8, traces hero, Nicolas Parris, 9.
Photograph © Rebecca Van Slyke 2008

Rube Goldberg

July 4, 1883–December 7, 1970
Cartoonist, Illustrator

Cartoonist Rube Goldberg [GOHLD-burg] is so famous that his name has its own definition in Webster's Collegiate dictionary, which says: "A RUBE GOLDBERG is a machine that does some easy task in a very complex or silly way." Goldberg started drawing fantastic inventions to make fun of the way people complicate things. His contraptions go through many steps and use elements like monkeys, explosions, and melting ice to do simple jobs like sharpen a pencil or shut a door. Goldberg studied to be a mechanical engineer but became a cartoonist and sportswriter instead. He started with a San Francisco newspaper in 1904 and worked until his retirement in 1964, bringing enjoyment to his readers for 60 years. Goldberg will be remembered for the creative humor in his amazing "time-saving" inventions.

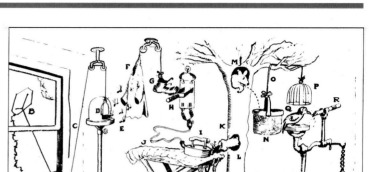

Professor Butts gets his think-tank working and evolves the simplified pencil sharpener.

Open window (**A**) and fly kite (**B**). String (**C**) lifts small door (**D**), allowing moths (**E**) to escape and eat red flannel shirt (**F**). As weight of shirt becomes less, shoe (**G**) steps on switch (**H**) which heats electric iron (**I**) and burns hole in pants (**J**).

Smoke (**K**) enters hole in tree (**L**), smoking out opossum (**M**) which jumps into basket (**N**), pulling rope (**O**) and lifting cage (**P**), allowing woodpecker (**Q**) to chew wood from pencil (**R**), exposing lead. Emergency knife (**S**) is always handy in case opossum or the woodpecker gets sick and can't work.

Rube Goldberg |*Simplified Pencil Sharpener.*
Rube Goldberg is the ® and © of Rube Goldberg, Inc., www.RubeGoldberg.com

Invent a *Rube Goldberg*

Look on the Internet or in library books for Rube Goldberg cartoons to enjoy with their inventive style and sense of humor. Then design and draw a contraption with interrelated impractical steps. Steps can be labeled with A, B, C action.

Materials

drawing paper
choice of marking pens, colored pencils, or crayons

Process

❶ Draw a machine that will:
- tie a shoelace
- peel an orange
- turn on the TV
- wash dishes
- open a can
- pet the dog
- throw a touchdown
- do any simple job!

❷ The drawing should show many steps, all of them silly and completely impractical, each step causing something to happen that leads to the next step and to the next until the end result is finally achieved.

❸ Label each step with a letter, starting with A on the beginning of the drawing (left side) and ending with the finished task and a final letter (right side). Under the drawing, write a description for each lettered step in the style of classic Rube Goldberg cartoons.

Automatic Breakfast Machine
by Nici Smith, 11.

Pulling the lever on circus cannon (A) fires a giant cork (B), which hits spring platform (C), tossing a one-pound weight (D) onto a platform (E). The weight knocks loose a small red ball (F), which rolls down a long shoot and lands on the handle of fork (G), flipping chicken feed (H) across to a chicken (I). The weight pushes the platform down, so a giant hand (J) tickles the chicken on her back, causing her to lay an egg (K). The egg rolls into frying pan (L), gets cooked, and becomes a delicious breakfast (M).

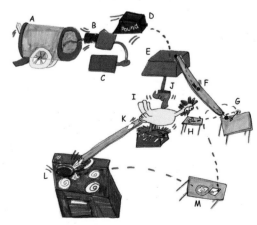

Grant Wood

This pretty white house with a Gothic window is the actual house that Grant Wood used as the model of the farm house in his famous painting.
Photograph courtesy of John Langholz, St. Louis. All rights reserved.

February 13, 1891–February 12, 1942
Regionalist painter, All-American

Grant Wood was born on a farm near the small town of Anamosa, Iowa. His love of the farm was to become the focus of his paintings, which began an important style of art called All-American. Grant showed an interest in art at a very early age, drawing pictures with burnt sticks his mother gave him from her wood stove. He loved his farm chores and had his own goats, chickens, ducks, and turkeys. When Grant Wood grew up, he painted the scenes of the people and farmland he knew so well, as important as anything he had seen anywhere. His most famous painting is called *American Gothic* showing a farmer and his daughter standing before an arch-shaped Gothic window. Grant liked the contrast of the fancy Gothic window on a plain American farmhouse. He painted his family dentist and his own sister, Nan, as models for a farmer and his daughter. Some people thought Wood was making fun of farmers; others thought he was honoring them. When Grant Wood painted *American Gothic*, he was simply making a painting of the people he had known all his life.

American Gothic Singers, Girl by Holli Howard, grade 1, *Boy* by Gregory Woody, grade 1.
Art courtesy of April Barlett, art teacher, Richmond, Virginia, Photo by John Langholz

Gothic Paste-Up

Invent characters to pose in front of a photograph of the actual house Grant Wood used as the model for his famous *American Gothic*. Wood painted a farmer and his daughter, but with your imagination, create new people, animals, or imaginary characters. Include their outfits or props to hold. Humor is encouraged! Cut and paste the new characters into the Gothic house scene. To see Grant Wood's famous *American Gothic* painting, go to www.artic.edu.

Materials

print-out of the photograph of
    the *American Gothic* house
    (color or black-and-white)
8½ by 11-inch drawing paper
drawing tools: colored pencils,
    pens, crayons

scissors
glue or gluestick
construction paper
pencil
ruler

Process

1. Print out the house photograph from www.brightring.com.

2. Draw two characters in a size that will fit into the photograph scene. Some suggestions are:

aliens	animals	toys	insects	yourself
children	elves	athletes	friends	Seussels (p. 60)

3. Grant Wood gave his farmer a pitchfork. Add details to the characters that give clues about them, unique things to wear or hold. Humor and fun are encouraged. For example, draw a cat with a bird on its hat, apple-people with legs and arms, aliens from a giggly green planet, or a fuzzy mouse husband and his lovely cat wife. Anything goes!

4. With scissors, cut out the characters. Position them on the house print-out and glue in place, making sure the famous Gothic window can be seen. If they are too big, it's OK to cut away some of the drawing to make them fit on the paper. When ready, dot a little glue on the back of each one and press into place.

5. To make a paper frame, cut away a center rectangle from a sheet of construction paper. Center the artwork in the frame, and tape or glue it in place.

American Art Explodes

Ellie, 4, sits on a rock outdoors while creating Jackson Pollock action art.

Photo © 2007 by Margaret Mahowald, Golden Valley, Minnesota.

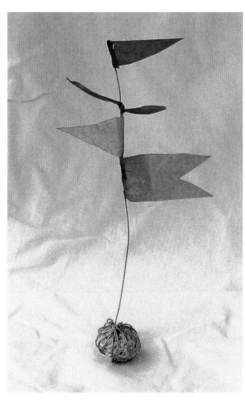

Tissue, wire, a few dabs of glue, and a small rock are the only materials needed to create an Alexander Calder-inspired rocking stabile.

Photograph ©2008 by MaryAnn Kohl

Red Cat in Collage by Rita Bespalova, kindergarten, in Romare Bearden's collage style.

Norman Rockwell

Norman Rockwell
Summary of cartoon, *Norman Rockwell at work.*

February 3, 1894–November 8, 1978
Illustrator, Romanticist

Rockwell [ROK-wel] is recognized by millions of Americans for his warm and humorous illustrations showing American life. The cover of the *Saturday Evening Post* was his art showcase for over 40 years, giving him an audience probably larger than that of any other artist in history. At age 19, Norman Rockwell began as the art editor of *Boys' Life*, where he was assigned to paint several of the magazine's covers. At 21, with help from the *Post* cartoonist Clyde Forsythe, Rockwell successfully published eight covers in 12 months. He went on to publish 321 more for the *Saturday Evening Post* over the next 47 years; he created over 4,000 original works. Many are in permanent collections, but many others were sadly lost in a devastating fire in Rockwell's studio. The *Four Freedoms* series was his personal favorite, symbolizing President Franklin Roosevelt's wishes for freedom in America. The Norman Rockwell Museum in Stockbridge, Massachusetts, owns and displays a collection of his paintings and has preserved his most recent studio for visitors to view. In 1957, the United States Chamber of Commerce in Washington, DC, cited Rockwell as a Great Living American, saying, "Through the magic of your talent, the folks next door—their gentle sorrows, their modest joys—have enriched our own lives and given us new insight into our countrymen." Norman Rockwell will always be a favorite great American artist. See Rockwell's art at the Norman Rockwell Museum website, www.nrm.org.

Magazine Cover

Using drawing tools of your choice, design and illustrate the cover art for a personally designed magazine. Give the magazine a name to print boldly on the cover art.

Materials

drawing tools: markers, crayons, paint, colored pencils, pastels
permanent marker in any bold color
ruler and pencil
colored paper, scissors, glue (optional)
digital camera or scanner, computer with graphics software, and printer (optional)

Process

1. Look at magazine covers for inspiration. Then, think of a unique, interesting new magazine idea. Here are some suggestions: *Ballet Highlights for Kids, Soccer Stars, Future Cooks of America, Neighborhood Animals, RazzleDazzle Sports, Outdoor Adventure, Best Books Ever, Travel Dreams, Colorful Art Fun, Best Desserts, Jokes and Puzzles, Our School News.*

2. Think of the things that are usually seen on a magazine cover: title, featured artwork or photo, titles of stories and features inside, date.

3. To begin, illustrate a magazine cover that expresses what the invented magazine is about or what stories or features might be found inside its pages. Use any choice of drawing or painting tools. Remember to include the name of the magazine! The name can be separate, or it can be illustrated right over the drawing. A pencil and ruler may be helpful for sketching out the cover before coloring or painting.

4. The name of the magazine may be added with bold permanent marker or may be painted or drawn in any way. Some artists may wish to add write-ups and additional pages to the magazine with such ideas as a feature story, news events, recipes, and advertisements.

Ranger Rita, by Nici Smith, 9

Computer Graphics Cover

Scan the illustration or use a digital camera to take its picture. Upload the illustration to the computer. When it opens in the photo/graphics program, add the name of the magazine with the text tool. Use any font or color that helps express the character of the magazine. Print out the illustration with the magazine's new name.

Pond Life, Design by Callie Winton, 6,
Art by Shannon Baker, 6

Ansel Adams

Ansel Adams | *Girl smiling (Occidental type)*, 1943.
Library of Congress No. LC-A35-6-M-4

Ansel Adams
Louise Tami Nakamura,
(youngest daughter), 1943.
Library of Congress No. LC-A35-4-M-30-B

Ansel Adams
Joyce Yuki Nakamura,
(eldest daughter), 1943.
Library of Congress No. LC-A35-4-M-19

Ansel Adams | *Kenji Sano*, 1943.
Library of Congress No. LC-A35-4-M-65

February 20, 1902–April 22, 1984
Photographer, Realist

Ansel Adams [AH-duhmz] is one of America's greatest photographers. He is best known for his magnificent black-and-white photos of California, the high Sierra Nevada Mountains, and the dramatic cliffs and waterfalls of Yosemite Valley. Adams was born in California. He received his first camera when he was a teenager on a family vacation to Yosemite National Park. Although he was studying to be a musician, his love of photography encouraged him into the wilderness and into the darkroom, where he developed his own photographs. Adams was a talented photographer, and people liked his work, which soon was shown in galleries and museums. His photographs and his conservation activities helped preserve many wild and beautiful places. During World War II, Ansel Adams traveled to the Japanese American Internment Camp in Manzanar, a small town in the California desert. Many Japanese American families were sent to prison camps like Manzanar during the war. Adams photographed life in the camp, documenting the hardships and positive spirit of the imprisoned people. The pictures from Manzanar are among Adams's best portrait photographs. You can see Adams's nature photographs at www.anseladams.com.

Friendly Portrait

Create a portrait by photographing a friend from different views. Then glue favorites to heavy paper for display. Encourage the friend to express herself with facial expressions, clothing, or special objects to hold. Expressing is the key to a fine portrait.

Nice to Meet You, Cody, 8

Materials

digital camera and printer (or a disposable camera with photo prints)
a friend to photograph
printed photos

scissors
glue stick
piece of mat board or sheet of heavy paper

Blue, Blue Smile, McKenzie Thompson, 8

Cowgirl Blues, Cristina Hernandez, 8

Process

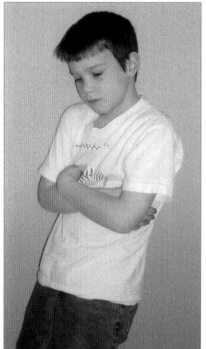

On My Mind, Brett Bovenkamp, 8

1. First choose a subject for your photographic portrait of an important person: a best friend, brother, sister, or favorite adult.
2. Get ready! Select lighting: The most successful natural lighting for portrait photos is outdoors on a sunny day in full shade. (Avoid dappled shade where leaves cast shadows and avoid bright sunshine.) Select a simple background: solid wall, fence, or side of a house.
3. Photo time! Take multiple pictures of the person. With a digital camera, take at least 12 to 24 pictures (with a film camera, use all the film on the roll). Get close enough so the face fills the camera's viewfinder. Photograph the friend from the front and from the side. Ask them to use facial expressions like smiles or serious or sad looks. They can choose to look however they are truly feeling.
4. Print out pictures on a printer with adult help or take the film to be developed. Save copies of the photos on the computer or save the film negatives. If there is a favorite photo, it can be enlarged.
5. When the photos are printed, choose several favorites. Arrange the chosen photos on a piece of mat board or heavy paper. Place them in neat rows or make a design and place them here and there.
6. Glue the photos in place and display the portrait of this special friend.

Alexander Calder

July 22, 1898–November 11, 1976
Abstract sculptor

Alexander Calder [KAWL-der], called Sandy by all who knew him, was born in Pennsylvania. Calder came from a very artistic family: his great-grandfather and his father were sculptors, and his mother was a painter. When Calder was young, he and his sister used to play with toys and gadgets that Calder made. When Calder grew up, he continued to create such things as games, toys, jewelry, sculptures, drawings, paintings, costumes, movie sets, mobiles, and stabiles. Through his construction of wire mobiles, he became the founder of a new art form—kinetic sculpture, which means sculpture that moves. His works from small to tremendous include mobiles (suspended moving sculptures), standing mobiles (anchored moving sculptures), and stabiles (stationary constructions). Calder is the most famous kinetic sculptor in the world. See Calder's sculptures at www.nga.gov.

Rocking Stabile,
kindergarten artist

Rocking Stabile

Arrange wires on and around a rock base, creating a stabile that is balanced and satisfying to view. For extra color and flair, add scraps of paper or collage items to the wires.

Materials

rock

wire: heavy or thin hobby wire, floral wire, pipe cleaners, or chenille wires

heavy-duty scissors or wire cutters (adult help required)

straight-nose pliers

paper scraps (patterned, plain, foil, tissue, colored)

collage items: buttons, sequins, yarn, colorful thread, fabric pieces, stickers, confetti

glue, tape, or stapler

Process

❶ Select a rock to use for the base of the stabile that sits well without wiggling or tipping and is appealing in size, color, shape, and texture. To find a rock, go for a walk around the school, the neighborhood, along a wooded path, in a park, or anywhere rocks can be found. Beaches, rivers, or creeks have excellent rock selections.

❷ Bend and wind a piece of heavy wire around the rock, allowing a long piece of the wire to stand up from the rock. This will be the strong and central part of the rock stabile. Other wires can depend on the strong central wire.

❸ Add another piece of wire to the rock stabile by twisting to attach. Continue adding wires in any design and shape. Think about the balance of the sculpture so it will stand and not fall over. Wires can be moved and bent as needed.

❹ When the stabile is in balance and satisfying to view, the mobile is basically complete. However, some artists may wish to add "flags" of paper scraps or other collage materials to the wires. To do this, snip bits of paper scraps (choose by color, texture, pattern, shine). Fold a scrap over a wire and glue, tape, or staple in place. Stickers are easily applied as well. Add as many scrap flags as desired. Other collage materials can be added as desired. Buttons will thread on pipe cleaners and wires, as will large sequins.

❺ As a final step, adjust wires and flags so the standing rock mobile balances well. Wires can be moved and bent to encourage balance. When finished, look at the rock stabile from different views, turning it this way and that. Choose a favorite view for display.

Walt Disney

December 5, 1901–December 15, 1966
Theme Park Designer, Animator

Walter Elias Disney [DIZ-nee] grew up on a Missouri farm, where he showed talent in drawing, selling his first sketches to neighbors when he was only seven. Walt constantly doodled pictures of animals and nature and showed a talent for performing. Walt Disney became an animator, theme park designer, film producer, director, screenwriter, voice actor, entrepreneur, and philanthropist. He is most famous as the creator of animated characters such as Mickey Mouse, Minnie Mouse, and Donald Duck, to name a few! Disney's dream came true with the opening of Disneyland Park in 1955, which he designed and founded. Later came Walt Disney World Resort, Magic Kingdom Park, Epcot, Disney's Hollywood Studios, Disney's Animal Kingdom Park, and Disney's California Adventure Park. Walt Disney once said, "You can design and create and build the most wonderful place in the world. But it takes people to make the dream a reality."

Williams World, by Jehue, 5, and Elijah, 3

Playground Model

Draw/invent a dream playground. Then construct a model of it on a salt-dough base, adding playground equipment and details with paint, paper, plastic, string, sticks, and more.

Materials

paper and pencil
Salt Dough: 2 parts flour, 1 part salt, 1 part water
Large square of sturdy cardboard or plywood
items for building the model playground: paper, string, yarn, ribbon, small tiles, sticks, straws, bottle caps,
bamboo skewers, yogurt cups, craft sticks, cotton balls, Styrofoam trays, wood scraps
tape: regular, masking, duct
glue, stapler
sand, glitter
toy figures
tempera paints
paintbrushes

Process

1. To begin, draw an imaginary playground on paper, viewed as if looking down on a map. Show pathways, fences, walls, pools, trees, water, grottos, or other imagined features. Draw areas for playground equipment, and if ready, draw the equipment itself. (Or draw equipment later.)

2. Prepare the Salt Dough in a big bowl. Dump the dough on the square base of cardboard or plywood. Press and smooth it to cover the entire surface right up to the edges, about 1-inch deep for flat areas, thicker for raised areas. Refer to the drawing plan. Mound, mold, or press into the dough any pathways, pools, ponds, or hills to match the drawing. Feel free to improvise.

3. While the dough is still damp and soft, begin building the playground equipment from the materials and scraps. This could take quite a while! Firmly press the pieces right into the dough. Add trees or bushes, cacti, rocks, or other objects to complete the playground. The dough should be soft the following day, but by the third day, it will be rock hard. At that point, glue will be required.

4. Let everything dry. Paint the map dough in any way, highlighting pathways and borders. To make grass or gravel, dab glue in specific areas, and then sprinkle with colored sand or glitter. Green sand looks like grass, and blue glitter makes a pond or pool sparkle.

5. When everything is completely dry, add toy figures to "enjoy the park" and make it look, as Mr. Disney would say, like the "happiest place on earth."

Charles Biederman

Charles Biederman | #24, *Constable*
Designed September 1977, created 1979. Collection of the Frederick R. Weisman Art Museum, University of Minnesota, Minneapolis, Biederman Archive, Gift of Charles J. Biederman.

August 23, 1906–December 26, 2004
Constructionist sculptor

Karel (Charles) Joseph Biederman [BEE-der-muhn] was born to immigrant Czech parents in Cleveland, Ohio. Biederman was interested in art from an early age and attended classes in figure drawing and watercolor painting as a teenager. As a young man, he was an apprentice for a local ad agency. Charles Biederman was a painter and sculptor who became well known in New York City in the 1930s for his geometric paintings and aluminum reliefs depicting his belief that art comes from nature. Nature played a part in how Biederman chose to live; he resided in virtual isolation for most of his adult life in Red Wing, Minnesota, with his wife, Mary, and daughter, Anna. There he climbed the hill behind his home every day to sit and think about nature and all its wonder. What he saw in nature, he brought to his art. It is said that near the end of his life, he had a card on his desk that read, "At last I am one with nature."

Edgy Relief

Biederman used aluminum in his art, but young artists can design a relief using scraps of wood or posterboard glued standing on thin edges. If no wood scrap is available, use cardboard, posterboard, mat board, or tagboard rectangles and shapes. Even an old deck of cards will do with a little extra glue-dry time.

Materials

wood scraps (plain, painted, or dyed with liquid watercolors or food coloring)
posterboard
white glue

glue gun (optional, with adult supervision)
glue-dots (optional, require dexterity)
scissors

48

Process

❶ Spread the variety of scraps out on the workspace to see the shapes. Experiment with standing them on edge to see if they will stand unaided. The ones that balance easily will work best, but all scraps are workable.

❷ Stand some of the scraps on their edges on the background posterboard in a design. Move them around and explore different design ideas, turning them this way and that, spacing them into different patterns. Because the scraps will fall over, let them stay where they fall until they are needed.

❸ When ready, begin gluing the center scrap of the design first. Glue other scraps moving outward from the middle. Some scraps will need to be held in place until the glue takes hold.

❹ Let the entire relief dry overnight.

❺ Display the work on a wall, like Biederman's art, or on a table, shelf, or other flat surface.

Relief Color Techniques

• Natural or Painted Wood: Use plain or natural wood scraps to build the relief. Paint the scraps when the glue of the relief has dried, or leave natural.

• Metallic: Spray the entire relief with metallic spray paint. All the scraps and the background will be the same color.

• Sparkly: Dust the relief with powdery glitter or further decorate with sequins or confetti.

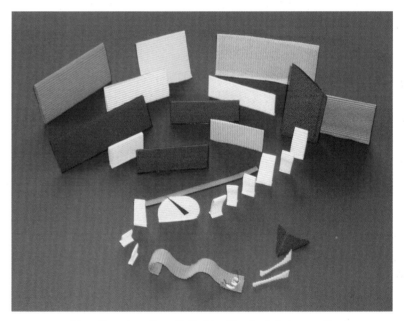

Blue Construction Relief, by Frederick Jones, 6, cardboard on posterboard

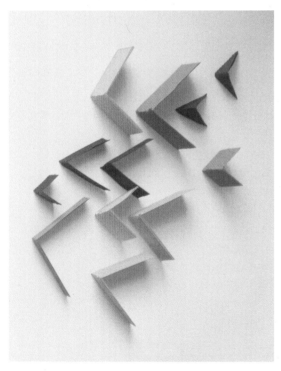

Yellow Construction Relief, by Frederick Jones, 6, cardboard on posterboard

Mark Rothko

September 25, 1903–February 25, 1970
Abstract Expressionist painter

Marcus Rothkowitz (Mark Rothko) [ROTH-koh] was a Latvian-born American painter and printmaker who is classified as an Abstract Expressionist, although he rejected not only this label, but even being an Abstract painter. The Rothkowitz family moved to Portland, Oregon, when Marcus was 10 years old, and that is when he shortened his name to Mark Rothko. When he grew up, Rothko moved to New York City to attend classes and begin his art career. He began painting his famous color-field pieces in 1947, developing his well-known style of large rectangular fields of color stacked one above another. He used variations on this format for the rest of his career. His later paintings often consist of soft-edged luminous colorful rectangles floating on enormous canvases. Rothko once explained, "I am not an abstract painter. I am not interested in the relationship between form and color. The only thing I care about is the expression of man's basic emotions: tragedy, ecstasy, destiny." Rothko believed that all paintings should be miraculous. You can see Mark Rothko's art at www.metmuseum.org.

Color-Field Panel

Paint a large color-field on a large sheet of cardboard. Then paint soft-edged "floating rectangles" on the color-field.

Materials

very large sheet of card-
board, 3 by 6 feet or larger
tempera paints, thinned
pencil
tempera paints

wide paintbrush
sponges, cloths, rags
paint roller (optional)
large sheets of colorful art
tissue paper (optional)

Process

❶ Choose two or three colors that inspire or bring emotion: happiness, sadness, silliness, anger, and joy are a few. Sometimes certain colors just feel right or satisfying. Choose what feels right or inspires emotion.

❷ Stand the cardboard up against a wall with newspapers under it to catch drips. If an easel is available, stand the cardboard up at the easel. To paint the color-field, paint the entire sheet of the cardboard with one color. Use sponges or rags to apply the paint thinly to avoid leaving any visible brush strokes. More than one color may be used, but the colors should blend in hue and not be in contrast. Let this color-field sit until almost, but not completely, dry.

❸ When the cardboard is almost dry, take a pencil and lightly sketch huge floating rectangles on the color-field. Two or three stacked rectangles will be most like the style of Rothko, but any individual expression of size or shape is fine.

❹ With a sponge, cloth, or wide paintbrush, paint the rectangles with tempera paint in a chosen color. More colors may be blended into the rectangles to give them variation in hue. Keep the appearance of the edges soft.

❺ For added interest, press a large rectangle of art tissue into the wet rectangle of paint. It will stick without glue. A paintbrush damp with water will press the paper into the paint.

❻ Stand back and look at the work. If it needs more paint color blended in, this is the time to do it. Then let the large work dry overnight.

Painted Rectangles and Tissue, by
Anna-Maria Bruscatto, 6

Willem de Kooning

April 24, 1904–March 19, 1997
Abstract Expressionist painter

When he was 22 and living in Holland, Willem de Kooning [d' KOO-ning] stowed away across the ocean on a freighter to Newport News, Virginia, then eventually found his way to New York. De Kooning made his living briefly as a house painter and then as a commercial artist before committing to being a full-time artist. He was an important leader of Abstract Expressionism and was labeled an "Action Painter" (see Jackson Pollock, p. 56, and Mark Rothko, p. 50). His mid-career was marked by the use of abstract slashes of color and expressive brush strokes. In the 1980s, his paintings became beautifully simplified, and in 1990, he painted his last work. De Kooning's paintings continue to be appreciated and collected by people around the world. See Willem de Kooning's art at www.moma.org and www.guggenheim.org.

Wall of Intertwining Ribbons

On the largest paper possible, paint intertwining ribbons of color with different sizes of brushes and choices of color. Use large arm movements to make connected designs that cross over one another.

Adult supervision required

Materials

background paper: white craft paper (on rolls from hobby or art stores), butcher paper, large sheet of plywood covered with white latex paint
masking tape (push pins, optional)
newspaper
container of water

brushes: small, medium, and wide, including a large house-painting brush or sponge brush
tempera paints in individual containers
large wall space
step stool (optional)

Process

1 Prepare the paper. Roll out a long piece of craft paper on the floor. Use as much as desired. Then roll another panel the same length right next to the first, edges touching. Tape the two sheets together with a long piece of masking tape. A third or fourth panel can also be rolled and taped to the first two. When all the panels are seamed together with tape, turn the paper over so the tape is on the back.

Willem de Kooning working on an unfinished stage of *[untitled]*
oil on canvas, 70 × 80 in, East Hampton, New York, 02/02/84. Photograph by Tom Ferrara, courtesy of The Willem de Kooning Foundation, Artwork © The Willem de Kooning Foundation/ Artists Rights Society (ARS), New York

2 Tape or tack the paper to a large blank wall with the bottom of the paper at the edge of the wall where it meets the floor. Adult help and a step stool or ladder will be helpful. Spread newspapers on the floor beneath the hanging paper to catch drips. To avoid need for a ladder or stool, the paper can be painted while on the floor and hung on the wall later.

3 Mix the tempera paint to a smooth, flowing (but not runny) consistency. With a choice of paintbrushes, stand before the large canvas and begin to paint a swirling ribbon of color. Use large arm movements and body action, pushing down on the brush to make wide lines and letting up on the brush to make light or narrow lines. A step stool or ladder may be necessary to reach the highest parts of the paper.

4 Change colors and brush sizes, and then paint another swirling ribbon that intertwines or crosses over the first. Continue with ribbons and designs with choice of colors and brush widths. Spots, blops, and dots are effective to add. Fill the huge paper until satisfied. Then let dry. Stand back to view the intertwining art.

Barbara Cooney

Barbara Cooney
Illustration from *Chanticleer and the Fox* by Geoffrey Chaucer
Scratch art, approximately 8 × 6 in © 1958 by Thomas Y. Crowell Company, Inc.
Used with permission of HarperCollins Publishers. All Rights Reserved

August 6, 1917–March 10, 2000
Illustrator, Folk artist

Barbara Cooney [KOO-nee] and her twin brother were born in Brooklyn, New York, in Room 1127 of the Bossert Hotel. As Barbara grew, her artist mother encouraged Barbara's childhood art. Barbara Cooney described her mother's guidance saying, "My mother gave me all the materials I could wish for and then left me alone, didn't smother me with instruction. Not that I ever took instruction very easily! My favorite days were when I had a cold and could stay home from school and draw all day long. My mother was an enthusiastic painter of oils and watercolors. I could mess with her paints and brushes all I wanted. The only art lesson my mother gave me was how to wash my brushes. Otherwise, she left me alone." After Barbara Cooney graduated from college, she knew she wanted to be an artist and illustrate children's books. She has said that three of the books (*Hattie and the Wild Waves*, *Miss Rumphius*, and *Island Boy*) are like an autobiography of her life. Her first illustration work used etching and scratchboard techniques. Barbara Cooney received two Caldecott Awards (for *Chanticleer and the Fox* and *Ox-Cart Man*), the highest award for children's book illustration. She has created some of the most beautiful and important children's books of all time, having illustrated over 100 in all. She said that a picture book is like a string of beads with the illustrations the jewels and the text the string that holds them all together.

Scratchboard Illustration

Barbara Cooney's earliest design and illustration works were done entirely on scratchboard. Scratchboard is a clay-coated board on which black ink is applied. White lines and areas are scratched or scraped off the board with sharp-edged tools. Explore Barbara Cooney's scratchboard technique on precolored hobby scratchboard. Enjoy reading all of Barbara Cooney's books!

Materials

precolored scratchboard from a hobby, craft, or art store

sharp-edged tools for scratching and etching: opened paper clip, plastic darning needle, large nail, cuticle stick (orange stick or pointed wooden stick), wooden dowel (sharpened in pencil sharpener), tips of scissors, wooden scratching tools, fingernail

Process

❶ Begin scratching away a design into the scratchboard. As lines are etched in the black board, colors that are underneath will appear.

❷ Continue scratching until the design is complete.

Homemade Scratchboard

Color over a square of mat board or posterboard with bright, heavy crayon. Then, paint over the crayon with black tempera paint with a little liquid dish detergent mixed in. When dry, scratch designs the same way as described above.

Scratching Tools

Today's hobby, art, and craft stores have scratchboard in varieties of colors. Some come with child-safe scratching tools specifically designed for younger children.

Scratchboard Tree in Gray, Gold, and Red,
by Kristen Abel, 11

Multi-Colored Butterfly Etching,
by Nici Smith, 9

Scratch & Etch Leaf, by second grade artist

Buckminster Fuller

R. Buckminster Fuller | Montreal Biosphère, 1967
Montreal, Canada, Steel and acrylic cells, 76 m diameter × 62 m high (200 × 200 ft).
Photograph by © Michael Plante

July 12, 1895–July 1, 1983
Architect, Inventor

Buckminster Fuller [FUHL-er] was a unique architect and inventor who spent his life trying to make the world a better place for people. Bucky, as he was known, was born in Massachusetts and spent summers on an island farm off the coast of Maine, where he loved to make things out of old junk, play with boats, and invent things. Later, Fuller went to college at Harvard, a famous American university, but was asked to leave twice for not doing his schoolwork. He joined the navy and later worked as a workman and machine operator. Bucky could not find success in any of his jobs. In 1927, when his young daughter died of an illness, he blamed himself for being poor and unable to provide for his family. But then he began to think of his life as an experiment to discover what a penniless, unknown person might be able to do for the betterment of mankind. Fuller designed buildings that were strong, cheap, and useful. Fuller went on to develop some of the most remarkable ideas in the entire world: new ways to make buildings, cars that conserved energy, games and maps to teach world unity and peace, and his most famous invention—the geodesic dome, a round building built from triangles. The remarkable thing about a geodesic dome is that the larger the dome gets, the lighter and stronger it becomes. Since the invention of the dome, all kinds have been built for sports arenas, airports, stores, and homes. It is hard to label Buckminster Fuller. He has been called an architect, inventor, scientist, engineer, mathematician, educator, philosopher, poet, speaker, author, futurist, and designer. He is all these and a great American artist.

Tetrahedra Sculpture

Buckminster Fuller turned flat triangles into three-dimensional shapes that were very strong. Explore creating tetrahedra with soda straws and yarn. Optional ideas include decorating the sculpture with glue and colorful paper, stickers, or magazine cut-outs. One shape is a tetrahedron, and several shapes together are tetrahedra.

Materials

plastic drinking straws (non-bending)

large, plastic yarn needle (plastic sewing needle with a blunt point, sometimes called a tapestry needle, darning needle, or child's craft needle)

3 feet of yarn or string

white glue

pencil

scissors

colored papers: tissue paper, construction paper, gift wrap, colorful magazine pages

Process

Building a Tetrahedron

❶ A tetrahedron is a shape with six edges and four sides. Each tetrahedron needs six soda straws to construct. First, drop the threaded yarn needle through three of the straws. Tie a knot, making a triangle out of the straws. Do not cut the remaining yarn.

❷ Using the same yarn, string two more soda straws. Tie the yarn at one corner of the first triangle. Now there are two triangles making a diamond shape with a line across the middle.

❸ Work the yarn needle through one of the straws so the yarn comes out on one of the diamond points. A thin piece of wire may be needed to push the needle and yarn through that straw, since it might be a tight fit.

❹ String one more soda straw onto the yarn. Pull the other point of the diamond up and tie a knot. This is a tetrahedron! Cut the yarn.

❺ Several of these shapes are called tetrahedra (not tetrahedrons). Construct as many as desired for the tetrahedra sculpture.

Decorating a Tetrahedron

❶ Lay one side of a soda-straw tetrahedron down on a piece of colorful paper. Trace around it. Cut the paper on the traced lines. Squeeze a thin line of glue onto three of the straws in the tetrahedron and carefully set it down onto the cut-paper triangle. Give it a minute to dry a bit, then lift it up. Now one face of the tetrahedron is decorated with paper!

Julia Odegaard creates one tetrahedron to eventually be joined into a tetrahedra sculpture.

Photo © Kim Solga 2008

❷ Cover a second face with another paper triangle. Leave the third face open to see inside the shape.

❸ Add stickers and cut-out magazine pictures to the paper faces of the tetrahedron. Glue them onto the paper walls inside and out. Use lots of different colors.

❹ Decorate the rest of the tetrahedra the same way. Work slowly and take breaks so the white glue has a chance to dry and become strong.

Assemble a Tetrahedra Sculpture

❶ One decorated tetrahedron looks great, but several tetrahedra glued together create a colorful and interesting sculpture.

❷ Glue the decorated tetrahedra face to face.

❸ Tie a piece of string on the point that will be the top corner and hang the sculpture from a hook on the ceiling.

Jackson Pollock

January 28, 1912–August 11, 1956
Abstract Expressionist painter

Jackson Pollock [POL-uhk] grew up in the western states of Wyoming, Arizona, and California. As a young art student, Pollock moved to New York to make his way in the art world. After studying with painters like Thomas Hart Benton (p. 38) and Mexican muralists, Pollock began to work in larger and larger formats. He invented a style of abstract painting using a very runny paint to cover large canvas panels spread on the floor. "On the floor I am more at ease," Pollock once said. "I feel nearer, more part of the painting, since this way I can walk around it, work from the four sides and literally be in the painting." Pollock used brushes, sticks, and even kitchen basters to drip and pour paint into creative patterns. His technique was called Action Painting. Pollock moved with his whole body as he painted, sometimes carefully dripping paint, sometimes swirling and flinging paint in swirls and webs of color. You can see Jackson Pollock in action at www.loc.gov.

Faith, 5, concentrates on her Jackson Pollock action painting created outside on large craft paper. *Photograph courtesy of Margaret Mahowald, Golden Valley, Minnesota*

Great Action Art

Recreate Pollock's painting style in a suitable outdoor spot, where splattered paint can be cleaned up easily. Spread large paper on the ground. Drip, fling, swirl, arch, splatter, sprinkle, spray, and pour paint in designs that fill the paper. Dress appropriately!

Materials

tempera paints, thinned some with water (other paints such as liquid watercolors work well)
tall containers to hold paint
large sheet of paper, at least 36-inches wide by 80-inches long
4 rocks as paperweights
painting tools: slender sticks (1- to 2-feet long), paintbrushes, kitchen baster, spray bottle, toothbrush
painter's tarp (optional)
water and clean-up supplies

Process

1. Spread the paper out on the flat ground with plenty of room to walk around. Place small rocks on the corners to hold the paper in place. (If working outdoors, work on a calm day.)

2. Pour paint into tall, skinny containers so tools can dip deeply.

3. Dip tools into paint and flip or drip the paint onto the large sheet of paper, just as Pollock did. Move around and around the paper. Add many different layers of color, weaving the drips, arches, swirls, and splatters of one color with another, using all the different tools. If several children are working together, take turns and supervise kids and their painting tools well. Limit painting groups to two to four children to keep paint under control. (Note: Each kind of tool used will distribute the paint differently. Small branches pruned from trees and stripped of leaves are thin and flexible, good for flinging or dripping. Use a handheld spray bottle for spraying, a toothbrush for splattering, and a kitchen baster for squirting.)

4. Let the completed action painting dry completely.

Saul Steinberg

June 15, 1914–May 12, 1999
Cartoonist, Illustrator

Saul Steinberg [STYN-burg] was born in Romania and arrived in America at the age of 28. He became an American illustrator particularly well known for the pictures he drew of people communicating. He began to record the way of life in the United States primarily through his work at the *New Yorker* magazine. Steinberg once said his illustrations only masqueraded as cartoons; he used the cartoon as a way to tell a story in one single funny or playful picture. All in all, Steinberg's work is mainly about communication of thoughts, ideas, and feelings. The drawings he made clearly illustrate communication, but not with words or letters; his characters communicate with squiggles and symbols. See Steinberg's cartoons at www.saulsteinbergfoundation.org.

Squiggle Talk

Draw a cartoon with pencil or black pen, and show the characters communicating without words, using only symbols or squiggles.

Materials

white paper
pencil or black pen
scissors (optional)

Process

❶ Look at some of Steinberg's cartoons in books or on the Internet to enjoy his unique ideas of how characters can communicate. Look at the cartoons drawn by other kids on this page to see how they have enjoyed communicating with squiggles and symbols.

❷ Cut white paper into squares about 8 inches by 8 inches. Each cartoon drawing will have its own white square of paper.

❸ Now think about symbols and lines that communicate. Swirls and loops say something different from jagged lines or bold dots. Hearts mean something different from lightning bolts. Exclamation points make a strong point!

❹ Draw one or two characters who have something to say. Then add their thoughts or feelings shown with symbols or squiggles.

❺ A cartoonist usually signs his or her name at the top or bottom of the cartoon. Do the same with a flourish.

Three-Eyed Alien Meets a Boy on a Swing, by Levi Butler, 10

Cats in Love, by BreAuna Rose Phair, 8

Romare Bearden

September 2, 1911–March 12, 1988
Expressionist painter, Photomontage

At age three, Romare Bearden [BEER-din] and his family settled in the Harlem neighborhood of New York City, where his father worked as a sanitation inspector and his mother was involved in the community and society. Music always filled an important place in Bearden's life. He grew up listening to jazz and the blues and was acquainted with many musicians, including his famous cousin, Duke Ellington. When Bearden grew up, he began a career in painting later than many other artists. His winding path as a great American artist was filled with varied employment, such as a cartoonist, musician, and mathematician. Bearden became well known in 1964 when he set aside abstract painting and began to work in collage. He is best known for his collage and photomontage artworks of city life, including his famous works of performing jazz and blues musicians. He produced approximately 2,000 works of art consisting of collage, paintings, drawings, monotypes, murals, record-album jackets, magazine and book illustrations, and set designs for theater and ballet. The overall importance of Bearden's collage-paintings feels musical. Bearden once said, "You put down one color, it calls for another. You have to look at it like a melody."

Romare Bearden | *Mother and Child*, ca. 1976–77
Collage on canvas mounted on masonite, 48 × 36 in. Image courtesy ACA Galleries, New York. Art © Romare Bearden Foundation/Licensed by VAGA, New York, NY

Baby Sitter, by Maria Vasquez, grade 3

Mixed Montage

A montage is the technique of producing a single artwork made from a combination of fragments of pictures, text, materials, film, or even music. Create a montage with photographs, paper, and fabric on fiberboard backing.

Materials

fiberboard or Masonite

collage materials: fabric scraps, newspaper, magazine clippings, greeting cards, foil, art tissue, comics, postcards, gift wrap, photographs, tape (masking, washi) foil paper

scissors

glue

sponge and water (optional)

paint, crayon, or markers

wide, soft brush

white glue, thinned with water in a dish or decoupage medium such as ModPodge

duct tape (optional)

Process

① Place the fiberboard sheet on the work surface. Any size sheet will do, from drawing paper size on up to extremely large. Select collage materials to suit the size of the fiberboard. Find photographs and magazine clippings that begin to have meaning for the collage, noting color and texture as well as image. Begin to arrange them on the board, moving them about without gluing.

② Cut pieces of fabric, foil, and other odds and ends. Paintings and drawings, or any materials, can be included. Arrange them all, moving the pieces around until satisfied with the arrangement. At this point, some colored washi tape or masking tape can also be added for color, texture, and design if desired.

③ Brush glue on the back of each item in the montage and press down to the board to hold in place. Optional step at this point: Take a damp sponge and remove or enhance the color of images by rubbing parts of an image with water. Work gently and slowly. This can give a

Night Music, by Maria Vasquez, grade 3

faded or shadowy effect to photos and clippings, or it can completely change the color of them. In addition, markers or crayons or paint can add color here and there. Sign the montage in one of the corners with a permanent marker, if desired.

④ Brush a coat of thinned white glue over the entire montage with a wide, soft brush, coating all of the work evenly. Some edges may require gentle brushing to help them lay flat. Let the montage dry several days, until hard and clear.

⑤ For extra permanence, cover all four edges of the work with silver duct tape, forming a frame. Pull the tape the entire length of the board's edges, letting the tape fold part way over each edge to the back.

Theodor Seuss Geisel

March 2, 1904–September 24, 1991
Illustrator

Theodor Seuss Geisel [GEE-zuhl], better known to the world as the adored and respected Dr. Seuss [soos], was born in Springfield, Massachusetts. His father and grandfather were brewmasters in the city. His mother raised the children and is often credited with helping the Geisel children fall asleep with soothing rhymes and chants from her childhood. Dr. Seuss says his mother gave him the ability and desire to create the rhymes for which he became so famous. Geisel, an American writer and cartoonist, is best known for his classic children's books written under the pen name Dr. Seuss, including *The Cat in the Hat*, *Green Eggs and Ham*, and *How the Grinch Stole Christmas*. He wrote and illustrated 44 children's books in all, favorites of children and adults alike. Seuss said, "Children want the same things we want. To laugh, to be challenged, to be entertained and delighted." That's exactly what his books with strange and imaginative characters have done—entertained, delighted, and inspired millions of children to learn to read. Dr. Seuss was honored with two Academy Awards, two Emmy Awards, a Peabody Award, and the Pulitzer Prize. But his greatest contribution to the world is his delightful art with unique, memorable, and enjoyable characters.

Dr. Seuss drawing the Grinch.
World Telegram & Sun photograph by Al Ravenna, 1957, Library of Congress LC-USZ62-124309

Seussels

Create a new character for a children's book or a cartoon using imaginative touches like Dr. Seuss. There is no limit to the possibilities when Dr. Seuss is inspiring the art room!

Materials

crayons or other drawing tools
sheets of white paper

stapler (optional)
black marking pen or pencil

Process

1. Draw an animal-type character or a person-type character or maybe an animal-person character! Where imagination is concerned, there is no limit. One eye, two eyes, three eyes, four. Draw some eyes and draw some more! Blue hair, green hair, yellow, or blue. On the moon or in the stew.
2. If interested, draw the character in a story that has sequence and action over several pages. Staple the pages together like a book. Design and draw a cover with a title for the story, if interested.
3. Some artists will want to make up a story or silly rhymes for the drawings. Write them on the drawing or have someone else write them down.
4. Name the new cartoon character something unique, catchy, or humorous.

Bunny Bird, by Ashely, 8

Feathered Rabbit, by Sammie VanLoo, 8

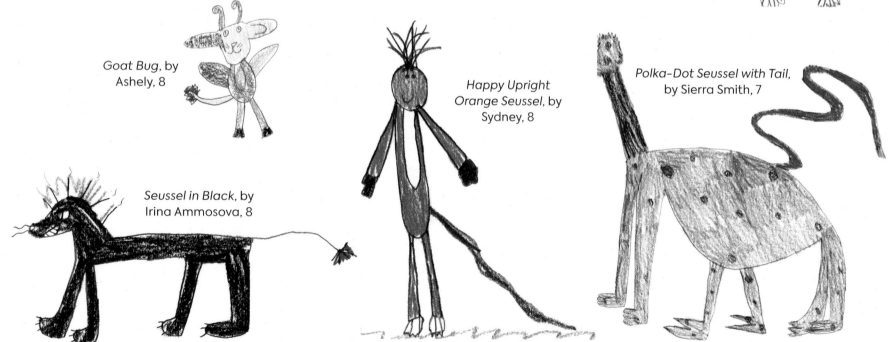

Goat Bug, by Ashely, 8

Happy Upright Orange Seussel, by Sydney, 8

Polka-Dot Seussel with Tail, by Sierra Smith, 7

Seussel in Black, by Irina Ammosova, 8

Wolf Kahn

Wolf Kahn | *In the Gloaming*, 2002
Pastel. Permission to reprint courtesy of the artist, photograph by Peter Muscato,
Art © Wolf Kahn/Licensed by VAGA, New York, NY

October 4, 1927–
Abstract Expressionist painter

Wolf Kahn [kahn], born in Stuttgart, Germany, came to the United States at the age of 12 and eventually came to be regarded as one of America's greatest and most influential landscape painters. In the late 1940s, Kahn studied painting at the famous Hans Hofmann School in New York City (p. 28), where other well-known painters also studied. In the 1950s, Wolf Kahn emerged as a painter of Abstract Expressionism. His art evolved into landscape painting of intense light and color. Kahn's art expresses nature in a new way through works that are sometimes soft and luminous and other times bold and intensely colored. Kahn would like young artists to know that he uses tissues, paper towels, and his fingers to move his soft pastels around on the paper, applying one color on top of another. He says, "The art I made as a child are some of my most prized possessions."

Layered Soft Pastel

Explore the application of soft pastels on drawing paper while creating a landscape or other design. Use tissues, paper towels, and fingers to move and work the colors on the paper. Try Kahn's technique of applying one color on top of another, creating layers of blended and interacting color.

Materials

white drawing paper
pencil (optional)
pastels, soft variety (Kahn rec-
ommends Rembrandt brand
pastels)

blending tools: paper towels,
tissues, fingers
hairspray or hobby coating
(optional)

Process

1. Decide to work freehand or to lightly sketch with a pencil first. Create either a free-form design or a landscape. The landscape can be imaginary or based on an actual landscape seen out the window, on a walk, or from photographs.

2. Begin by working pastels gently onto the paper, blending, smearing, blurring, or smudging the colors as desired with paper towels, tissues, or fingers. Add one color of pastel on top of another. Continue working with a choice of blending tools to soften or intensify color.

3. Try to fill the entire sheet of paper with color. Don't worry about the color being true to nature. Pink rivers, orange skies, blue leaves, and purple grass are part of the fun of creating, expressing, and exploring with pastels.

4. When the pastel work is complete, it can be smudged easily, so place it in a folded sheet of very smooth paper for carrying. If displaying, position the artwork on a wall away from where shoulders and elbows might bump into the drawing.

Smudge Control

Hairspray or spray hobby coating may be lightly used to help control the smudgy nature of the pastel drawing but will darken the color. Use with adult supervison.

Douglas Fir Forest in Chalk, by Madeline VandeHoef, 8

Sunflower, artist unknown, grade 3

Forest Fire Tree, by Cody, 8

Richard Diebenkorn

Richard Diebenkorn | *Ocean Park #54*, 1972
Oil on canvas, 100 × 81 in, San Francisco Museum of Modern Art, Gift of Friends of Gerald Nordland, Catalogue Raisonné #1469. © Estate of Richard Diebenkorn

April 22, 1922–March 30, 1993
Abstract Expressionist painter

Richard Diebenkorn [DEE-ben-korn], born in Portland, Oregon, and raised in the San Francisco Bay area, was a versatile artist who expressed himself through several styles, including Representational, Abstract, and Abstract Expressionism. His abstract *Ocean Park* series, created over 20 years, contains 140 paintings called *Ocean Park*, named for the neighborhood where his art studio was located. Each painting has the same name but each one is different—and yet somehow the same as the others. The *Ocean Park* paintings do not show scenes that look like trees or houses or streets, but they are still pictures of these things. They are paintings of the colors and textures Diebenkorn saw in his town, arranged into abstract designs. Diebenkorn believed in *pentimento*, an Italian word meaning that the composition or designs in an artwork could change during the process of painting. Diebenkorn valued discovery and change in his paintings, something children who paint can value as well. Diebenkorn is known as a master of composition. He arranged lines and shapes on his canvases so that people just naturally like the patterns he created. His paintings are beautiful and powerful works of abstract art.

Stain Painting

Though Diebenkorn didn't paint with this staining technique, it's an interesting way to explore the look of his *Ocean Park* series. Arrange art tissue on paper, paint over the tissue with water in a soft brush, and then peel away the tissue to reveal a watercolor-stained abstract.

Materials

art tissue scraps and sheets or crepe paper
scissors
water
paintbrushes

large white or pastel paper or white posterboard
white glue, thinned, or acrylic gloss medium (optional)

Process

1. Cut or tear colorful art tissue into strips or other shapes. Strips from crepe paper rolls can also be used.
2. Arrange the tissue shapes or strips on the background paper, letting them cross over each other so they will blend and blur.
3. When ready, paint water over the tissue, soaking pieces thoroughly and causing them to bleed and stain the paper. Colors will mix and blur with each other.
4. Peel away the wet paper pieces to reveal the finished abstract design.
5. Dry completely.
6. The painting may be brushed with white glue thinned with water or brushed with acrylic gloss medium to give the finished work extra shine.

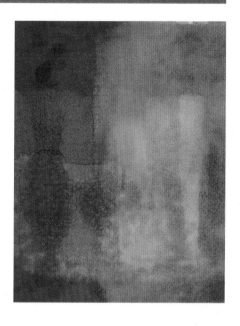

Diebenkorn Stain Paintings,
all by Ilana Pechthalt, 9

Jasper Johns

May 15, 1930–
Post-Abstract Expressionist painter

Jasper Johns [jahns] spent his childhood in South Carolina, where he often lived with relatives, moving here and there from town to town. He began drawing as a child and by the age of five, knew he wanted to be an artist when he grew up. During his 20s, while living in New York City, he made the decision "to stop becoming an artist and actually be one." One night, he had a dream that inspired him to paint the American flag. He began to paint other symbols, such as targets and numbers. Johns's paintings were different from other Abstract Expressionists of the time because they were simple, cool, unemotional, and impersonal pictorial images, instead of wild and explosive expressions. A painter, sculptor, and printmaker, Jasper Johns is most recognized for his pictorial images of flags and numbers. Jasper Johns is one of America's best-known Post-Abstract Expressionists. See Jasper Johns's famous *Flag* at www.moma.org.

Encaustic Flag on Wood

Design and paint a flag on wood with melted crayon, a method called encaustic, similar to the technique used by Jasper Johns.

Adult supervision required

Materials

pencil
6-inch by 12-inch smooth scrap of wood
electric warming tray or electric frying pan set on warm and lined
   with heavy aluminum foil
crayon stubs (broken, peeled, sorted)
old, stiff paintbrushes

Process

① Plug in the electric warming tray. Allow it to heat while beginning step two. An adult should always supervise carefully around heat and electricity.

② With a pencil, draw a flag design on the wood scrap. The flag can be imaginary or based on an actual flag like the American flag in red, white, and blue. Sketch in the design with a light touch. Most of the lines will not show later.

③ Place peeled crayon stubs on the warming tray in little piles, separated by color. Let the stubs melt into soft puddles or mounds. This will be the paint palette.

④ Dip a paintbrush into the warm melted crayon, and quickly move to the wood to paint the colored wax into the flag design. The crayon will harden as it cools, so work quickly. The brush will stiffen as the wax cools in the brush. Move the brush back to the warming tray palette and dip into more melted crayon, repeating the painting step. The brush will soften as it warms once again. Change colors as needed. Paint the entire piece of wood until the flag is complete. (To clean the warming tray, simply wipe with paper towels while still warm.)

Encaustic Flag on Wood,
third grade student

Andy Warhol

August 6, 1928—February 22, 1987
Pop Art painter

Andy Warhol [WAR-haul] is America's favorite Pop artist, best known for his colorful images of celebrity faces and everyday products like soup cans and soda pop bottles. He was born the youngest son of Czechoslovakian immigrant parents. He was very shy and often sick when he was a child, and he had a very hard time at school. But his incredible artistic talent helped him get through college and move to New York City to become a great American artist. For many years he worked as a commercial artist, designing advertisements, magazine illustrations, and greeting cards. Warhol created portraits of things that were popular in America. He painted the well-known faces of movie stars like Marilyn Monroe and Elizabeth Taylor, and political figures like Chairman Mao from China. He painted products that Americans saw and used every day like cans of soup. He added his own fantastic colors to realistic drawings, and he is known for repeating objects and designs over and over.

Andy Warhol | *Small Torn Campbell's Soup Can (Pepper Pot)*, 1962
Casein, gold paint, and graphite on linen, 20 × 16 in, Courtesy of The Eli and Edythe L. BroadCollection, Los Angeles. © Andy Warhol Foundation for the Visual Arts / ARS, NY /TM Licensed by Campbell's Soup Co.

Package Design

Everyone has a favorite soup, candy bar, drink or packaged food. With markers and drawing paper, design the packaging for a personalized food product or alternative healthy choice.

Materials

white drawing paper
pencil and eraser
colored marker pens
suggested fun food package
 (as a model): soup, cereal,
 bread, cake mix, crackers,
candy, soft drink, chips,
pasta, take-out box, frozen pizza, dried fruit snack,
frozen vegetable box, salad mix container

Process

1. Select a favorite packaged food and use its wrapper, box, or object as a model. A photograph or picture from a magazine advertisement will also work.
2. Sketch the package shape on drawing paper, working larger than life-size, filling the paper from side to side.
3. Personalize the drawing by substituting your own name into a part of the label. For example, Megan's Sweet Bar chocolate candy, Edward's Cola soda pop, Kelly's Cocoa Krispies, or Hannah's Organic Wheat Bites. Keep the recognizable style of the package, reproducing the same type of lettering when adding the label. If the product or food does not have a label or packaging, invent one!
4. When the pencil sketch is finished, color the product portrait with marking pens, matching the colors of the package or using new, surprising colors.
5. Cover an empty box or can with a custom label for added creativity.

Bean 'n' Bug Soup, by Rebekah Butler, 11

Wayne Thiebaud

*November 15, 1920–
Pop Art painter*

Wayne Thiebaud [TAY-boh] is a California artist best known for his paintings of yummy food. Thiebaud's first wish was to be a cartoonist because he loved classic cartoons and comic strips. When he was a soldier in World War II, he created a comic called *Wingtips*. Before he became a painter, he worked as a commercial artist in advertising and briefly as a cartoonist for Walt Disney Studios. Many of Thiebaud's most famous paintings from the 1950s show common objects from American life like rows and rows of cakes and pastries that might be seen in a cafeteria or bakery window. He painted cakes, pies, donuts, gumball machines, toys, hats, sandwiches, and plates of pancakes. Thiebaud's paintings show simple shapes, shadows, thick brushstrokes, and strong colors. Thiebaud didn't stop with cakes and pies. His paintings of San Francisco streets and California river landscapes are vividly colorful and so realistic that many look like abstract patterns. Pop Art became an important movement in America in the 1960s, and Thiebaud's cake paintings inspired other artists to look at common objects in new ways.

Wayne Thiebaud | *Bakery Counter*, 1962
Oil on canvas, Courtesy of Barney A. Ebsworth, private collection. Courtesy of Barney A. Ebsworth 2008,
Art © Wayne Thiebaud/Licensed by VAGA, New York, NY

Yummy Cake Painting

Cakes are pretty and delicious, reminding people of trips to the bakery, of munching goodies at a favorite restaurant, or of birthday parties and festive celebrations. Using watercolors, paint a yummy cake or other delicious object that includes real food extracts or flavored powdered mixes. Candy sprinkles add texture and color.

Materials

sheet of heavy white paper
pencil and eraser
watercolor paints and a paintbrush
food extracts or flavorings, such as vanilla, peppermint, or almond
flavored powdered mixes, such as cherry Jell-O or lime Kool-Aid
edible candy sprinkles
white glue

Process

1. Draw a cake on the heavy white paper. It might help to look at a cookbook or magazine with photos of real cakes or look at one of Thiebaud's artworks. Draw the cake big enough to fill the sheet of paper, and keep it simple. Thiebaud used basic shapes like circles, ovals, and triangles. He didn't fill his food art with backgrounds or people.
2. Fill several different containers with water for painting. Put a different flavoring or mix into each container. Add a drop of vanilla to one, a drop of mint to the next, a spoonful of cherry Jell-O to another, and so on. The painting water mixtures will smell delicious, just like a real dessert, but only for painting, not eating. Fragrances will help inspire the creation of big, yummy slices of cake or other desserts.

Yummy Cake Watercolor, by Cedar Kirwin, 12

3. Use watercolors mixed with the scented waters to paint the cake drawing. Don't drink the water—it's only for inspiration!
4. After the painting is finished and has dried completely, squeeze some white glue onto the frosting and filling areas of the painting. Shake candy sprinkles onto the glue and let it dry.

Real Cake Art Celebration

The best inspiration for a Thiebaud art project is to have a real cake as the model. The cake model can become a delicious celebration dessert when the painting is complete!

Roy Lichtenstein

Roy Lichtenstein | *I...I'm Sorry!*, 1965–66

Oil and magna on canvas, 60 × 48 in, Courtesy of The Eli and Edythe L. Broad Collection, Los Angeles. Photography by Douglas M. Parker Studio, Los Angeles, Courtesy of the Roy Lichtenstein Foundation © Estate of Roy Lichtenstein

October 27, 1923–September 29, 1997
Pop Art painter

Roy Lichtenstein [LIK-tuhn-stine] grew up in New York City. He studied art in college until he was drafted to fight in World War II. After the war, he returned to the United States to complete his graduate studies and teach art. Lichtenstein was part of the Pop Art movement of the 1960s. He had a long career as a painter, a printmaker, and a sculptor. His work used ideas and images from comic books, consumer advertising imagery, and art history. Lichtenstein's early Pop Art paintings are huge comic book–style pictures, such as exploding fighter jets and brokenhearted girls. He used black lines, primary colors, and Benday dots to mimic the contour lines, palette, and half-tone effect of the original comic strip. He would sometimes add speech balloons like the comic books to show what a character was saying or thinking. Speech balloons float above figures' heads and add dialogue to the story. Roy Lichtenstein also used action words in his paintings and liked to illustrate them in bold colors like red or yellow outlined in black to imitate the idea of a sound effect. Some great examples in Lichtenstein's works are WHAAM!, BLAM, BLANG, and VIP!

Comic Sounds

Invent and illustrate a comic sound word, place it in a speech balloon, and draw the main character, person, or thing making that sound in an interesting way.

Materials

posterboard or large white drawing paper
pencil and eraser
colored markers
permanent black marker
examples of comic books or Sunday funny papers (optional)

Process

1. Think of a sound. This might be a loud sound, a soft sound, a nice sound, or a scary sound. There's no right or wrong way to spell comic strip sounds! Comic words can have strange new spellings, like *snikt*, *bamf*, and *thwip*. Traditional comic strip sound words are fun to illustrate too, like WHAAMM, VAROOOM, BLAM, TAKKA-TAKKA, or POW! For inspiration, look at comic books and find Lichtenstein's art on the Internet or in books at the library.

2. Draw a square on the posterboard or drawing paper that will be the frame for the cartoon. The bigger the better!

3. Inside the square, write the comic sound word. Use a pencil to sketch large, illustrated block letters, slanting across the paper.

4. Draw a simple sketch to show what or who is making this sound.

5. Add special effects to the word, such as explosion lines, lightning bolts, puffs of smoke, and rays of light. Draw lightly with pencil, working large and filling the square.

6. When the pencil drawing is complete, outline everything with a wide permanent black marker pen. Use smooth, strong lines.

7. Color the cartoon drawing with markers. Bring out the expression of the cartoon with color. For example, dark colors are mysterious and frightening; bright red shows excitement; and light pastel colors express peace and happiness.

Did You Know?

When a word imitates a sound, the imitation is called onomatopoeia (ON-uh-MAT-uh-PEE-uh), a great new word to use around friends and family!

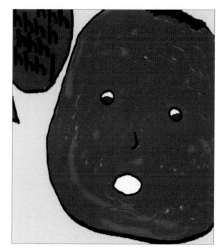

Hhhh!, Jordan Holstrom, 8   *Waa Waa!*, by Cristina Hernandez, 8

Beep! Vroom!, Sierra Smith, 7

Train, Madeline VandeHoef, 8

Robert Indiana

September 13, 1928–May 19, 2018
Pop Art painter, sculptor

Robert Clark was born in New Castle, Indiana. He later changed his name to Robert Indiana [in-dee-AH-nuh] and became known as a great American artist in the exciting and new Pop Art movement. When Indiana moved to New York City in 1954, he developed art he calls "sculptural poems" consisting of bold, simple icons or images, especially numbers and short words like EAT, HUG, and LOVE. Indiana's best-known image is the word LOVE with letters stacked in a square and a tilted *O*. The image was first created for a Christmas card for the Museum of Modern Art in 1964. In 1973, the US Postal Service put Robert Indiana's design on their very first Love Series postage stamp. Over 320,000,000 of these stamps were printed, delivering Robert Indiana's message to millions of people. Indiana said, "Some people like to paint trees. I like to paint LOVE. I find it more meaningful than painting trees." Robert Indiana thought that most people never stop to think about how beautiful words and numbers are. He said that he thought his job as an artist was "to make words and numbers very, very special."

Robert Indiana | *Love*, 1973
8-cent Love Stamp image reprinted with permission of the United States Postal Service. © Morgan Art Foundation Ltd. / Artists Rights Society (ARS), New York

Very Special Stamp

Design a postage stamp that highlights a special word or number. Work on normal-sized drawing paper. Then, if desired, reduce the stamp design to a small postage stamp size with a color copier or scanner. A postage stamp template to print out is available at www.brightring.com.

Materials

postage stamps, new or used, as examples
ruler or other straight edge
white drawing paper
scissors or craft scissors with wiggly edges
drawing tools: pencil, pen, colored pencils, colored markers, or crayons
color photocopier or scanner and color printer
paper and envelopes
glue or glue stick

Process

1. Look at postage stamps and become familiar with basic designs and borders. With a ruler and a pencil, draw a border around the white drawing paper. The border outside the line will stay white.

2. Think of special numbers or letters to draw on the white paper for a postage stamp design. Some special number ideas are your birth year, house address, allowance amount, or a favorite sports star's jersey number. Some special word ideas are happy, fun, Fido, snow, rose, Mom, or friend. Think of a word or number that is truly special. Lightly sketch the word or number in the drawing space. Fill the entire space. Make the letters thick or fancy in some way. Then outline the images with a pen, marker, or crayon. Don't forget to add

a money value to the stamp! Any amount is great, standard or imaginary. Color and decorate the design. Fill the background space with color and design.

❸ When done, cut the outer edge of the paper with scissors to make a wiggly edge just like a real stamp.

❹ With an adult's help, use a color copier or a scanner, computer, and color printer. (Note: Keep the large postage stamp design as the "master copy" or display later as art.)

Copier Method, One Stamp

Place the design on a color copier and reduce 90 percent. The resulting image will be about the size of a postage stamp, making one reduced play stamp. A postage stamp template is available at www.brightring.com to print out and use to create play postage stamps.

Scanner Method, Sheet of Play Stamps

Scan the design and reduce this image to about 1-inch square. Copy and paste this image over and over on a full-size page in a standard text document, filling the page. Then print on a color printer, making 50 to 60 pretend stamps. Adhere to an envelope with tape or glue.

Online Method, Sheet of Mailing Stamps

Upload a scan or photo of the original art to www.photo.stamps.com and create legal US Postal Service stamps to affix to your letters.

Write a Letter

For fun, write a letter to a friend or family member and seal in an envelope. Glue one of the homemade stamps on the upper right corner of the envelope. Deliver the letter secretly by hand. If you have an adult help you upload your stamp design to an authorized website (see Online Method), you can create official US postage that will allow you to mail your letter.

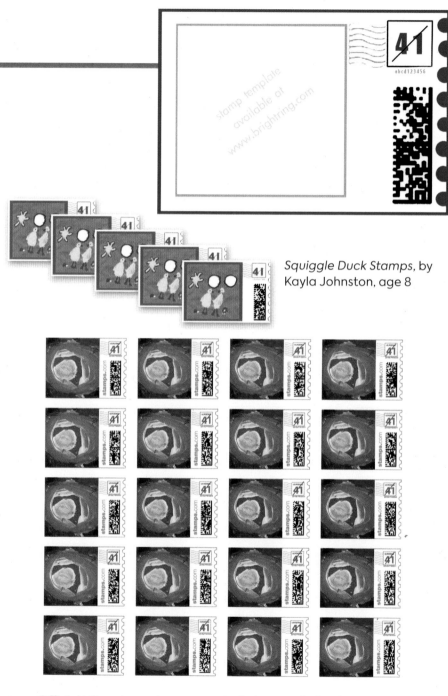

Squiggle Duck Stamps, by Kayla Johnston, age 8

Official US postage stamps created at www.photo.stamps.com, art by preschool student

Ruth Asawa

Ruth Asawa in her basement studio with one of the seven panels in this bas-relief.
Ruth Asawa, Renaissance Parc 55 Hotel, Motor Court Entry (dough panel), 1984. Photo by Allen Nomura, photograph courtesy of the artist

January 24, 1926–August 6, 2013
Expressionist sculptor

Ruth Asawa [ah-SOW-ah] was born in Norwalk, California, the child of Japanese immigrant farmers. During World War II, when Ruth Asawa was 16, she and her family were sent to an internment camp (see p. 44, Ansel Adams). Because America was fighting Japan, some people feared that all Japanese Americans could be a danger and had them imprisoned. Though American citizens, Asawa's family was forced to give up their freedom and home until the war was over. During her imprisonment, a family sponsored Asawa so she could attend college in Milwaukee. When the war came to an end, she went on to art school in North Carolina at Black Mountain College. After college in 1949, she headed to San Francisco to marry. Asawa became a great American artist, sculptor, and designer. As a mother, she was a strong supporter of art for children in the schools. Asawa worked with children to create baker's clay designs, then had the finished sculptures cast in bronze metal so the art would last for many years. In San Francisco, Ruth Asawa was called the "fountain lady" because her art decorates many fountains in public places. When Asawa created a fountain, she often used baker's clay, a flour-and-salt mixture, as her practice model. Asawa was best known for works of public art and wire-looped sculptures made from tied and twisted wire. To see more of Ruth Asawa's sculptures and other art, visit www.ruthasawa.com.

Ruth Asawa's Baker's Clay

4 cups regular white flour   1½ cups water
1 cup salt

Mix all ingredients with hands, squishing and kneading the dough until smooth. Bake finished dough at 250 to 300°F until hard, time depending on the thickness of the dough.

Dough Panel

Make Asawa's favorite baker's clay recipe and create a dough sculpture panel on a cookie sheet.

Adult supervision required

Materials

baker's clay (see recipe)
tools to use with clay: plastic knife, garlic press, rolling pin, wood
    cylinder block, chopsticks, plastic toy pieces, wooden block,
    kitchen utensils, table knife, fork, spoon
flat pan or cookie sheet
acrylic paints (optional)
acrylic varnish gloss medium (any hobby coating from craft stores)
paintbrushes

Process

1. Create a picture on a cookie sheet with the baker's clay. Roll it by hand and work it like clay. To begin, build a frame out of a long "snake" of dough, and place it on the cookie sheet. Next, fill in the frame with shapes and figures of dough. The artwork should be flat, about 1-inch thick. Work and build on the cookie sheet, joining dough pieces together. Dip fingers and dough pieces in water to help them stick together.

2. Table knives, forks, spoons, chopsticks, and plastic toy pieces make handy tools to shape the dough. Dough squeezed through a garlic press creates great clay hair. A rolling pin can flatten sheets of dough for backgrounds. Super-thin dough can be used as fabric draped over figures.

Dough Boy in Panel, by Devin Gartner, 9
Photograph ©2008 by Rebecca Van Slyke

3. An adult can bake the finished dough art in an oven at 250 to 300°F until hard. The time depends on the thickness of the art. It is recommended that the art bake until golden brown and hard, so that a spoon poked against the dough does not make a mark, or when tapped will make a hollow sound.

4. After the baked dough art is cool, paint it with acrylic paint, or leave it a natural dough color. It is important to brush on a coat of acrylic varnish or hobby coating to protect the dough from moisture.

Helen Frankenthaler

December 12, 1928–December 27, 2011
Abstract Expressionist painter

Helen Frankenthaler [FRANK-en-thaw-lur] grew up in New York City. Her love of art and paper began in childhood. She showed creative freedom in her artworks from her earliest years. Frankenthaler once saw Jackson Pollock's action paintings and was inspired to create her own new style of painting known as "soak stain." Frankenthaler would take large, plain canvas panels and pour liquid paint onto them, letting the paint puddle, run, and soak into the cloth. She worked on unprimed canvas, a textured cloth that would easily soak up the paint poured on top. Colors would float and soak into the cloth, thickening at the edges of puddles when the canvas was laid flat, mixing with other colors on the canvas, or dripping and flowing down when the canvas was slanted. She worked long and hard to create a painting and often threw away those she didn't like. Her successful color field paintings are large abstract compositions, glowing with areas of rich color. "A really good picture looks as if it's happened all at once," she said. Frankenthaler described herself as a "traditionalist and renegade." See Helen Frankenthaler's art at www.nga.gov.

Outer Space Map by
Anders Eiremo, 4

Soak Stain

Explore the soak stain technique using a heavy sheet of blotter paper that soaks up liquid tempera paint in interesting ways, a project best done in a well-protected work area or outdoors.

Materials

large sheet of blotter paper (office supply store) or heavy rice paper
sheet of cardboard, a little larger than the blotter paper
3 small paper cups (one for each color)
3 colors of tempera paints, mixed with water to syrupy consistency
large, soft paintbrushes (optional)
masking tape

Process

❶ Tape the blotter paper onto the cardboard. By taping all edges down with long strips of masking tape, the paper will dry flat and the masking tape will create a border when the tape is removed.

❷ Each artist will need three small paper cups, each containing a different color of paint. Limit the activity to three colors in the beginning, adding more colors with experience.

❸ Begin with the paper lying flat on the ground or on a protected work surface. Choose a cup of paint and pour a small pool of it onto the paper. Watch how the paint soaks in and what happens at the edges of the paint. Pour more paint and see what happens. Try pouring a trail of paint or narrow lines of paint, too.

❹ Select a new color, and pour a little of it next to one of the first paint puddles. Observe how the paper soaks up the second color and what happens when the colors meet. Notice how they mix together.

❺ Create an interesting design with careful, slow pouring of paint until the blotter paper is completely covered with color. Once a complete color field is created, the cardboard can be tipped slightly, if desired, so additional paint runs and flows gently down the paper. If desired, use a large, soft paintbrush to gently push pools of paint on the paper, like a mop spreading the liquid around, offering more control over the final design.

❻ Let paintings dry completely, usually overnight, before removing them from the cardboard. Carefully peel away the masking tape so the paper does not tear, revealing the frame left where the tape once covered the paper.

Agnes Martin

March 22, 1912–December 16, 2004
Minimalist painter

Agnes Martin [MAHR-tn] was born in Saskatchewan, Canada, and moved to the United States at the age of 19, living close to Bellingham, Washington, for many years. She became an American citizen at 38. In the beginning of her career, she worked only in black, white, and brown. At one time, she gave up painting and traveled around the West and Canada in a pickup truck and camper. A vision of an adobe brick inspired her to go to New Mexico where she built an adobe-and-log house on a mesa outside of the city limits. She began using light pastel washes in her grids. She once said, "When I think of art I think of beauty. Beauty is the mystery of life. It is not in the eye, it is in the mind." Martin is known as a Minimalist painter, though she preferred being called an Abstract Expressionist. She is known for her monochromatic (everything in one color range), geometric grid style that combines paint and light pencil lines. Martin's light, intriguing artworks use a minimum of color and design, which is where the term minimalist originates.

Agnes Martin | *Untitled*, 1994
Acrylic, 60 × 60 in, gift of the artist.Courtesy of the Harwood Museum of Art, Taos, New Mexico

Ruled Wash

Pencil lines are applied in a repeating grid fashion and then washed over with a light watercolor wash. The ruled grid may be further painted with a stamped block pattern.

Materials

large sheet of paper	plastic placemat
pencil	scissors
straight edge (ruler, yardstick, cardboard strip)	glue
	2-by-4 block of wood
thinned watercolor paint	slightly thin watercolor or tempera paint
soft, wide paintbrush	paintbrush
	scrap paper

Process

1. Use a straight edge such as a yardstick to draw a grid on the large sheet of paper. Make the lines cross the entire paper, forming rows and rows of lines. Draw this grid from top to bottom, covering the entire paper. The pencil lines will later show in the art.
2. Fill a soft, wide brush with the thin watercolor wash and apply the light color completely over the entire pencil grid. Set aside to dry. (If the paper curls or buckles, cover the painting with a sheet of newsprint and iron gently with a warm iron set with no steam to flatten the painting.)
3. Cut an old plastic placemat to fit the short side of a 2-by-4 scrap of wood (cut the placemat about 1½ by 8 inches). Then cut the placemat pieces into still smaller pieces.
4. Glue all the pieces onto the short side of the block of wood, soft side out. Set aside to dry completely.
5. When watercolor wash and the stamp are both dry, the artwork is ready for the stamp design. Paint the wooden block stamp with slightly thinned watercolor or tempera paint. Press the stamp onto a scrap of paper to see how it looks. Practice a few times.
6. Make stamp designs in rows and patterns across the paper, filling in the ruled grid in any way.

Agnes Martin, ca. 1954
Photograph by Mildred Tolbert, gift of the photographer. Courtesy of the Harwood Museum of Art, Taos, New Mexico

Elizabeth Catlett

Elizabeth Catlett
Education in Cuba, 1962
Linocut, 10-1/2 × 8-3/4 in, Image
courtesy of M. Lee Stone Fine Prints,
San Jose, California. Art © Elizabeth
Catlett / Licensed by VAGA, New York

April 15, 1915–April 2, 2012
Printmaker, Sculptor

Elizabeth Catlett [KAT let] was born in Washington, DC. Her parents were teachers, and she followed in their footsteps. She worked at a high school in North Carolina but left after two years because of the low salary she received as a black woman. She returned to college and became the first student to receive a master of fine arts in sculpture from the University of Iowa. One of her teachers was the great landscape painter, Grant Wood (see p. 40), who encouraged his students to work with subjects they knew best. Catlett's work began to focus closely on the lives of African American women. A few years later, Catlett traveled to Mexico to study woodcarving and ceramic sculpture. She worked with a group of printmakers in Mexico City who were creating art to promote social change. Catlett made block prints of black heroes and worked with other artists on posters and illustrations for textbooks and public art. She married Mexican artist Francisco Mora and made Mexico her home. Catlett created powerful prints and sculptures about the struggle for equality by poor and oppressed people everywhere.

Balsa Block Print

Draw and carve a design on the soft wood, ink it, and press onto paper. Tah dah—a print is made!

Materials

ballpoint pen and a dark crayon

white drawing paper, multiple sheets

balsa wood, in sheets (art supply store or hobby shop)

water-soluble printmaking ink or thick tempera paint spread on a plastic plate

brayer or a homemade ink roller

newspapers

Process

❶ Make a simple drawing on paper with a pencil, pen, or crayon. To transfer the design to the balsa wood, color all over the back of the drawing with a dark crayon. Next place the drawing on top of the wood. Hold it still. Lightly trace over the drawing's lines with a pen. The design will transfer as faint crayon lines to the wood beneath. Remove the drawing; it is no longer needed.

❷ Draw over the faint crayon lines on the wood with a ballpoint pen, pressing hard to make deep grooves in the soft balsa wood block. Drag or poke with the pen to create a variety of impressions, marks, and designs.

❸ To print the image, spread a little ink or paint on a plastic plate. Roll the brayer in the ink, covering the roller with a thin layer of ink.

❹ Place the balsa block, carved side up, on a sheet of scrap newspaper. Roll the inky brayer back and forth over the block, transferring color to the surface of the wood.

❺ Move the inky block onto a clean sheet of newspaper. Gently place a sheet of white drawing paper on top of the block. Hold the paper firmly with one hand while rubbing of the other with fingertips.

❻ Lift the edge of the paper slowly, and peel it off the block. The inked design (the block print) is now on the paper. Set it aside to dry.

❼ Make more prints using different colors of ink or paint and different types of paper. Make dozens to give to friends, to make into greeting cards, or to display.

Color Mixing: Colors can blend together in a rainbow effect by carefully rolling the brayer over two or three stripes of colors at the same time.

Jack-o-lantern: Balsa block (left) and print (right), by Nici Smith, 10

Georgia O'Keeffe

November 15, 1887–March 6, 1986
Expressionist painter

Georgia O'Keeffe [oh-KEEF] grew up on a farm in Wisconsin where she was recognized as a talented artist by the time she graduated from high school. Her family and teachers noticed her genius right away. She did not enjoy the traditional forms of painting that she learned in art classes, and she soon moved to New York City to explore new and different ways to create art. She became well known for paintings of gigantic flowers, seen very close up and filled with dramatic color. No one had ever painted flowers in quite this way before. In the summer, she traveled to New Mexico where she painted mountains and sunsets using her brilliant style. Eventually, she left the city to live on a ranch in the desert. She began to include bare sun-bleached bones found in the desert in her paintings. O'Keeffe lived to be nearly 100 and created amazing American art throughout her long life. O'Keeffe's art can be seen at www.imamuseum.org.

Painting with Distance

Georgia O'Keeffe made use of the natural curves and shapes of an object to create a larger-than-life painting. Paint blue sky and desert background. Then add a bone shape, which will appear close, with the background far off in the distance.

Materials

bone, piece of driftwood, or dry branch
paper, pencil, and eraser
large white watercolor paper
watercolor paints (tempera or acrylic paint also work)

paintbrushes
white drawing paper or beige construction paper
pastel chalks in grey, tan, and white
scissors and glue

Process

1. Choose a piece of a bone or dry wood as the subject for the painting. Bones can be saved from dinner, scrubbed clean, and dried. Driftwood can be found at beaches, lakes, and riversides. Smooth grey wood, where the bark has been completely worn away, is best for this project. Gnarly dry branches or a thick branch or root with many interesting twists and curves would also work well. Set aside the object until the background is complete.

Deer Bone with Distance, by Brett Bovenkamp, 8

2. Sketch a simple landscape with a high blue sky on the watercolor paper. O'Keeffe often showed distant hills with blue sky and clouds behind the bones of her desert paintings. The brilliant background would frame and peek through the holes and curves of the white bone. Paint the background landscape with watercolors. Fill the paper with color, and then let the painting dry several hours or overnight.

3. To add the foreground object, sketch the bone or wood onto a sheet of white drawing paper or beige construction paper, as large as the original painted paper or even slightly larger. Pastel chalks in light colors can be used to add subtle shading and highlights to the drawing.

4. Cut out the object and trim away all the background paper. Place the cut-out shape on top of the landscape painting. Move it this way and that, paying attention to the areas of painted background showing around and through the object. When these background, negative space shapes create a pleasant design, glue the object in place.

5. Trim any parts of the bone or wood drawing that hang over the edge of the landscape paper.

79

LeRoy Neiman

LeRoy Neiman, *Olympic Track*, 1976

Oil on board, original Serigraph image size 20 × 40 in.
Image courtesy of Knoedler Publishing, Inc. © LeRoy Neiman, Inc. All Rights Reserved.

June 8, 1921–June 20, 2012
Abstract Expressionist painter

LeRoy Neiman [NEE-muhn] was known for his brightly colored, semi-abstract action paintings. Most of Neiman's work focuses on sports, such as football, baseball, boxing, and even chess tournaments. "Concentrating on sports has helped me," Neiman once said, "because I couldn't refer back to past movements. There hasn't been any sports art to speak of . . . I've had the field pretty much to myself." His paintings are bold and colorful, with dashing brushstrokes and vibrant color. From the early 1960s, Neiman painted the athletes and events that Americans love best, making his work very popular. He caught the action of each sport, from championship games to the international spectacle of the Olympics. His paintings are reproduced as prints and posters, which make it possible for many people to own Neiman art.

Action Athlete

Action painting in the style of LeRoy Neiman is especially expressive for sports figures because it shows movement and action. In this activity, start with a photograph placed beneath clear acrylic. Then paint over the photograph on the plastic, focusing on dynamic brushstrokes and vibrant color!

Materials

large photos from sports magazines
acrylic paints (acrylic paints mix with water when wet, but not
    when dry; wash brushes before they dry.)
white dish or tray to use as a palette
masking tape
clear plastic sheets (office supply store)
small paintbrushes
water in a container for rinsing brushes

Process

1 Choose a photo of a favorite athlete in action. Select from gymnastics, football, dance, horse racing, NASCAR, baseball, track and field, bull riding, tennis, or another active sport. Find a large photo!

2 A white dish or tray with small squeezes of several bright acrylic paint colors will make a good palette. Include the primary colors—red, blue, and yellow—as well as white and black. If possible, add purple, green, and orange. The paints mix together easily to create every color imaginable.

3 Tape the sports photo onto a board or washable tabletop. Then tape a sheet of clear plastic over the sports image.

4 Mix the thick paint with a little water on the brush. Paint "LeRoy Neiman style" directly on the plastic with strong bold brushstrokes and colors brighter than real life. Paint the main figures in the photo, following the shapes and details visible through the plastic but using any colors desired. Paint the background and all the spaces around

and behind the main figures with bright colors. No need to stick to reality; use fantastic background colors like red, white, and blue, or bright purple and gold! Eventually, the painted picture will cover up the photo beneath. At this point, the photo can be carefully removed from under the plastic. The painting is complete, unless the Vibrating Line Effect step is followed.

Vibrating Line Effect: Paint Neiman-style action lines, which are small vibrating outlines that show movement and excitement!

5 Let the painting dry. Then peel tape away from the plastic, and stand back to see the action painting.

A young artist explores painting skateboarder Russ Milligan.
Original photograph courtesy of CitySkateboards, photograph of art by Kim Solga 2008

LeRoy Neiman, *The Rocket – Roger Clemens*, 2003
Oil on board, original Serigraph image size 27½ × 36 in.
Image courtesy of Knoedler Publishing, Inc. © LeRoy Neiman, Inc. All Rights Reserved.

Oldenburg & van Bruggen

Claes Oldenburg and Coosje van Bruggen | *Spoonbridge and Cherry*, 1985–1988

Aluminum, stainless steel, paint, 354 × 618 × 162 in, Collection Walker Art Center, Minneapolis, Minnesota, Gift of Frederick R. Weisman in honor of his parents, William and May Weisman, 1988 © Claes Oldenburg and Coosje van Bruggen

Oldenburg: January 28, 1929–
van Bruggen: June 6, 1942–January 10,
2009
Pop Art sculptors

Claes Oldenburg [klahss OLD-en-berg] and Coosje van Bruggen [KOH-sha vahn BROO-gun] were an art team who began their partnership with the large-scale sculpture *Trowel I* in the Netherlands in 1976. Since then, they created over 40 large-scale sculptures together. Oldenburg was born in Sweden, and van Bruggen was born in Groningen, the Netherlands. She received her art history degree from the University of Groningen and wrote many books on art and architecture. Oldenburg moved to America with his family when he was a small child and grew up in Chicago. In 1956, he moved to New York, where he became an important part of the Pop Art movement. Oldenburg is best known for his giant sculptures of everyday objects. He built huge sculptures out of cloth, vinyl, and fiberglass. He made giant toilets, typewriters, light switches, and fast food. He made a soft fabric and foam rubber hamburger big enough to sleep on; a four-foot-tall bacon, lettuce, and tomato sandwich; and a nine-foot-high hanging sculpture of giant French fries tumbling out of a paper bag! He created humor by making soft things hard or hard things soft, like a bathtub that drooped all over the floor. The size of his work made people smile. His later works, created in collaboration with his partner, Coosje van Bruggen, include many colossal-sized sculptures installed in parks and city plazas around the world.

Super-Size Sculpture

Making things much bigger than real life is a quality that Oldenburg and van Bruggen used in some of their sculptures. In this sculpture activity, a pair of dice is recreated on a much larger-than-life scale. The same process can be used to create other square items, while imagination can extend this process to objects of other shapes and textures.

Materials

2 large, square cardboard boxes (cubes, not rectangles)
scissors
white tempera paint
paintbrush or foam brush, about 2-inches wide
black or colored construction paper
white glue
newspapers
fishing wire and paper clips for hooks (optional)

Process

❶ Select two cardboard boxes that are each a cube, not rectangles. If the box is not already square, cut and fold the cardboard to create a perfect cube. An adult can assist young artists in this step.

❷ Place the boxes on newspapers and paint them with white tempera, if white dice are desired. Otherwise, use a different color like blue or red. Allow the first coat of paint dry completely, and if needed, add a second coat. Rest each box on balls of newspaper or blocks to raise it up off the floor to speed drying. Cut circles of black construction paper (or other colors if desired) to create dots to glue on the giant dice. Each side of the cube will have a different number of dots, from one to six. Glue them in place.

❸ To display, hang the dice from the ceiling using fishing wire attached to a corner of each die, and paperclips for hooks.

❹ For fun, scrap paper embellishments or fabric, foil, yarn, wire, and Styrofoam could be added to customize the dice sculpture.

Maddison Fox, age 8, shows off her large-scale dice sculpture.

Creativity with Boxes

Cardboard boxes can be the foundation for other giant sculptures, such as:

rectangular box ➡ giant brownie
rectangular box ➡ giant pink eraser, ends trimmed and folded
mailing tube ➡ extra large pencil or giant lip gloss
cardboard triangle ➡ huge slice of pizza
foil-wrapped cardboard shape ➡ huge chocolate candy "kiss"

Keith Haring

May 4, 1958–February 16, 1990
Pop Art, Grafitti artist

Keith Allen Haring [HAIR-ing] grew up in Pennsylvania as the only boy in a family with three younger sisters. Haring began drawing early in childhood. He would sit on his father's lap while his dad drew cartoons, and Keith would draw with him. Haring continued to draw and make art as he grew. At age 20, he moved to New York City, where he developed his unusual style and began his famous career. When he noticed empty black paper on the subways, he quickly bought white chalk and started making daily subway drawings. His work grew famous, though no one knew who was making the drawings. All the people riding the subway saw his work, and it was on TV and in the news. The drawings were bold and simple, in shapes like pyramids, flying saucers, winged figures, television sets, animals, and babies. Soon the baby icon with

Keith Haring's "crawling baby with radiating lines" is one of his most recognized art icons.

Keith Haring, *Untitled* (from the *Icons* series), 1990
Silkscreen, 21" × 25" © Estate of Keith Haring

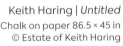

Keith Haring | *Untitled*
Chalk on paper 86.5 × 45 in
© Estate of Keith Haring

Haring's Favorite Kid Art Game

Keith Haring enjoyed working with kids. He described one project he liked to do: "I rolled out this big roll of paper. All the children sat around it. I'd do some drawings with markers or pens. I'd have music going and, as in 'musical chairs,' when the music stopped everyone moved to another part of the paper. When the music started, everyone continued to draw. It was a way of filling the paper in an interesting way. I've done this project in Japan, all over Europe and America—and it worked every time. It never got boring."

Photo by Elinor Vernhes
© Estate of Keith Haring

radiating rays became Keith's "tag" signature. Haring wanted everyone to be able to buy his work, so he opened a store called the Pop Shop to sell his art on posters, buttons, T-shirts, and games. Haring liked doing good things and worked with children in schools and made paintings and sculptures for schools and hospitals. In 1988 Keith became very ill, but he was brave and kept working hard until he passed away. Keith Haring's works can be found in museums, books, on posters and TV, and on his special kids' website, www.haringkids.com, with hundreds of Haring-style art ideas for kids to enjoy. Haring always insisted that children be a part of his appearances around the world, and he led creative workshops with them. Keith Haring always said, "What I like about children is their imagination." Keith wanted everyone to make art, especially children.

Subway Chalk

Keith Haring created drawings on the chalkboards of New York City's subways that made people smile and brought him fame and admiration. Create subway drawings with white chalk or paint on black paper and hang them on the wall. Add Haring's famous "radiating rays" to your design.

Materials

white chalk or white paint and a brush
large sheet or roll of black paper

Process

1. Work with white chalk or white paint on black paper to create a drawing in Haring's style. The lines should be bold and simple. Add radiating rays, lines, lightning bolts, or squiggles to show movement and action.
2. Use few details and broad cheerful lines.
3. Display the drawing on the wall, and see how people react when they see it.

Subway Chalk in Yellow, by Kristen Hopkins, age 10
Courtesy April Barlett, art teacher, Arthur Ashe Elementary School, Richmond, Virginia

White Paint on Black Paper, by two preschoolers

Haring Poses

Create a full-body pose that is traced on a large white paper roll. Outline with thick black marker or paint, adding Haring-style bold radiating lines. Fill in the posed shapes with one bright chosen paint color.

Robert Smithson

Robert Smithson, *Spiral Jetty*, April 1970, Great Salt Lake, Utah
Black rock, salt crystals, earth, red water (algae), 3½ × 15 × 1,500 ft. Image courtesy of the James Cohan Gallery, New York, DIA Center for the Arts, Photo by Gianfranco Gorgoni Art © Estate of Robert Smithson/Licensed by VAGA, New York, NY

January 2, 1938–July 20, 1973
Land Art sculptor

Robert Smithson [SMITH-sun] created land art or "earthworks," which are large sculptures built of rocks and dirt in outdoor locations. Smithson is best known for the *Spiral Jetty*, a huge ridge of rock that sticks out into the Great Salt Lake in Utah. This sculpture was partly inspired by the Great Serpent Mound, an ancient Indian monument in southwestern Ohio. Using black rocks and dirt, Smithson designed a coil 1,500 feet long by 15 feet wide that stretches out from the lakeshore. Sometimes the lake covers the jetty entirely. Other times the rocks stick up, and the mineral-and-algae-laden water creates different colors on the inside and outside of the jetty. Smithson was both an artist and a writer. He created artwork out of materials such as mirrors, maps, dump trucks, abandoned quarries, hotels, rocks, and dirt, creating sculpture, photographs, films, and earthworks. He was still a young man when he died in a plane crash while surveying sites for a sculpture he called *Amarillo Ramp* in Texas.

Spiral Earth Art

A spiral is a form or design found in nature as well as in man-made art. Starting from a point in the center, the curved line wraps out and around itself in a growing circle. Smithson chose a spiral shape for his famous *Spiral Jetty* art in Utah. Create a spiral work of earth art with a choice of natural materials, like sand, leaves, or snow.

Materials

approved outdoor location: ALWAYS ASK PERMISSION BEFORE CREATING LAND ART
natural materials: sand, leaves, snow, gravel, grass
tools: shovel, rake, hands, bucket, hoe

Process

Beach Spiral
Starting on a smooth area of beach sand, begin in the center, pushing up a ridge of sand. Use hands and sand tools to scoop and smooth the sand. Shape the ridge into a curve and continue curling the curve around its center in an ever-growing spiral.

Snow Spiral, Melting by Niles Alden, 6

Leaf Spiral
Rake fallen autumn leaves into a spiral design. One artist might build a spiral in a backyard or other leafy area, while a group of artists can work together to cover a much larger space, like a ballfield or an open meadow in a park.

Snow Spiral
The same process, using snow shovels and brooms, can transform a field of newly fallen snow into a work of art. Shovel and push snow into a long, curving spiral-shaped pile. As the snow melts, the curling spiral shape will appear even more dramatically on bare ground.

American Art Onward

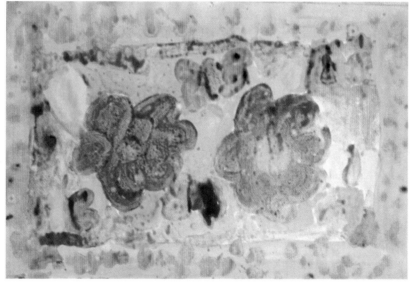

Target Paint by Morgan Marshall, 6, inspired by Frank Stella

Flower Diptych by Two by Sammie VanLoo, 8, inspired by Joseph Raffael

Foil Man Greeting by Katie Martin, grade 4, inspired by Roy De Forest

Photograph courtesy of Jeryl Hollingsworth, teacher

Roy De Forest

February 11, 1930–May 18, 2007
Funk Art sculptor, painter

Roy De Forest [dee FORE-ist] was born in North Platte, Nebraska, during the Depression and was the son of migrant farm workers. He grew up in Nebraska, Colorado, and eastern Washington. De Forest is best known for his richly colored, fanciful landscapes and worlds, canine creature paintings, and scrap-metal constructions. De Forest said, "For me, one of the most beautiful things about art is that it is one of the last strongholds of magic." He also felt that his art was a way to build a miniature cosmos where all his friends, animals, and paraphernalia could retire. His colorful spirited world of animals and people has a folklike quality that appeals to many people. Because of the junk he used in his art in the 1950s and '60s, he is said to be a pioneer of the Funk Art movement, a classification De Forest did not especially

like. The California Funk style of art is typified by creations with lighthearted subjects and outrageous wit. When De Forest was an art professor at USC-Davis, he continually told his students, "Create art that makes you happy," which is exactly what he did. Roy De Forest said that his own art amused him very much.

Roy De Forest, *Dog*, 1985, two views
Aluminum, paint; 24 × 8 × 28 in, Sylvia Elsesser, private collection.
Image courtesy of the Museum of Craft and Folk Art, San Francisco

Foil Friend

Construct a fanciful animal, creature, or friend from a taped newspaper form covered with heavy aluminum foil. Finish with dabs of paint and optional decorative materials. Roy De Forest is well-known for his dog sculptures, but any imaginable creature or "friend" will do.

Materials

newspaper
heavy tape, such as duct, masking, or packing
base material: cardboard, flat wood scrap,
   mat board, framing scrap, old cookie sheet
heavy-duty aluminum foil

paints and brushes
decorative materials (optional): ribbon, dog
   collar, faux fur, buttons, googly craft eyes,
   earrings, necklace, glitter, sequins, sewing
   trim, yarn, string

Process

❶ Build a strong underlying form for the foil sculpture. To do this, begin by rolling newspaper into tubes or rolls, taping securely to make them strong and stiff. These rolls can then be worked to form a body and appendages for the foil friend. Decide how many legs, arms, and heads it will have, and what posture or stance it will have; keep adding newspaper to form features. Add scrunched balls of newspaper too.

❷ Wrapping the form with lots of tape will make it strong and able to stand on its own. The form can stand on a piece of cardboard or other firm base. Tape it in place.

❸ Begin wrapping big sheets of aluminum foil around the form, covering it completely with several layers. Form the foil into ears or lumps and shapes that finish the friend's features and details. Cover the base with foil, if desired.

❹ Dab paint color here and there to add highlights and interest to your friend. It is not necessary to paint the entire foil sculpture—paint does not stick well to foil in large amounts, so sparingly is better.

❺ To further decorate, add ribbons, googly eyes, or other decorative items to bring out and complete the friend's unique fanciful personality.

Foil Men: Two Squeeze Poses by Katie Martin, grade 4
Photograph by Jeryl Hollingsworth, teacher

Fritz Scholder

October 6, 1937–February 10, 2005
Neo-Expressionist painter

Fritz Scholder grew up in North Dakota and Wisconsin as a typical American child who learned drawing and painting at school. Like most Americans, his family came from many different backgrounds, but the culture that eventually claimed Scholder's art was his grandmother's Native American heritage. Scholder studied art in college, exploring Pop Art and Abstract Expressionism. When he moved to New Mexico in the 1960s and began painting the real Native American faces of Santa Fe, the hardships of native people's lives and histories soon found their way into Scholder's artwork. His portrait paintings are some of the most powerful images ever created of American Indians. Scholder's most famous works are rich with color and simple, almost abstract, shapes. "Find out who you are and fully accept it," Scholder said. "You must be yourself on purpose."

Foam Brush Faces

Each young artist can release unique colorful creativity in a portrait painting based on the style of Fritz Scholder. Foam brushes allow paint to be spread in thick, smooth fields on mat board, with details added later with a smaller paintbrush and paints.

Materials

foam brushes from a hardware store, 1- and 2-inch widths
tempera paints, mixed to thick-syrup consistency
large white 11 × 17-inch mat board or heavy drawing paper
pencil and eraser
small paintbrushes
paper towels

Snake Face,
Kim Pinkley, 12

Flower Face,
James Zeller, 10

Process

❶ Using pencil, lightly sketch an imaginary face and shoulders. Make the drawing large, filling the paper. Use simple outlines and shapes and lots of imagination. Add unusual features and unreal special effects.

❷ Paint the background areas first. Select bright colors and use a wide foam brush. Rinse the brush well under running water at the sink between colors, and squeeze it dry with a paper towel. Keep paper towels and water handy for clean up.

❸ Then paint the skin, the hair, and the clothing of the figure. Again use a foam brush, and again paint large, solid areas of pure color.

❹ Set the painting aside to dry before adding details, if desired.

❺ Take a close look at several Fritz Scholder paintings for inspiration. Paint the details with a smaller, regular paintbrush. Paint eyes, nose, and mouth. Paint stripes and patterns. Let creativity run wild and paint flowers for hair, squares eyes, spirals, and zigzags.

Heritage Painting

Incorporate heritage in a portrait painting using a picture of a person from one's cultural background. Choose one culture from the many that make up one's family heritage. Using pencil, lightly sketch the face and shoulders similar to the person in the source photo. Then paint with bold colors using foam brushes and smaller brushes.

Sandy Skoglund

September 11, 1946–
Surrealist, Installation photography

Sandra L. Skoglund [SKAWG lund], born in Weymouth, Massachusetts, is an American photographer and installation artist. Her images blend surreal photography, sculpture, and installation art. Sandy Skoglund is known for creating tableaux—fantastic elaborate sets and scenes including actors, in oddly bright or contrasting colors—which she then photographs. Her tableaux can take many months to create. One of her best-known photographs of a tableau is *Radioactive Cats*, filled with green-painted clay cats running about a gray kitchen, where actors are part of the scene. Another piece, called *Revenge of the Goldfish*, features flurries of goldfish hanging above people in bed late at night. Sandy Skoglund is a master of imagination. She currently teaches photography and art installation multimedia at Rutgers University in New Jersey.

Sandy Skoglund | *Radioactive Cats*, 1980
Offset, 65 × 81 cm, Courtesy of the artist © Sandy Skoglund 1980

Surreal Tableau Photo

A tableau is a group of models or motionless figures representing a scene from a story. Set up a surreal tableau scene with chosen props, background, and supplies. Next, add toys or people as the actors. Then photograph.

Materials

tableau props: table, chair, sofa, desk, soccer ball, basketball, boxes, containers, plastic tubs, dishes, cups, pillow, blanket, bike, wagon, flowers, plants, party favors, holiday decorations
actors or objects to pose, such as: friends, classmates, parents, neighbors, relatives, siblings, dolls, action figures, toys, pets
location: room, corner, stage, patio, deck
costumes for actors or toys: hats, makeup, wigs, dress-up clothing
digital camera

Process

❶ Think of a tableau or scene to prepare and assemble. Something silly or surreal will be fun. Think of a scene that is opposite of real life, like a daddy dressed as a baby or a teddy bear costumed as an astronaut. Create with the materials and props on hand.

❷ Set up the props in the scene. Paint or prepare other background materials. For example, paint cardboard boxes or arrange blankets and pillows as background sets. Anything goes!

❸ Arrange the toys or real actors within the scene in costumes or in everyday clothing. Simple costumes are achieved with hats. More complex costumes can be put together from dress-up clothes, uniforms, or Halloween outfits. Makeup, wigs, glasses, scarves, shoes, and capes can add to the fun.

Surreal Tea Party: Unusual Friends in Unusual Places, Isaac Dykstra and Sydney P., 8
Photograph © MaryAnn Kohl 2008

❹ When the scene looks complete and everyone is holding still, take a picture with a camera. Take more than one picture, moving and rearranging props and toys or actors as needed.

❺ When the pictures are printed, choose a favorite, and frame with a simple paper mat.

91

Joseph Raffael

Joseph Raffael | *Spirit*, 2006
Watercolor on paper, 60 × 85 in, (JR06x4) © Joseph Raffael 2006, Image courtesy of the Nancy Hoffman Gallery, New York

February 22, 1933–
Realist painter, Contemporary

Joseph Raffael [ra-FAY-ell] was born in Brooklyn, New York. His mother, two older sisters, and aunt were the constants in his life. He says of his childhood, "I lived a solitary childhood, was often ill, and developed my own inner world; nature was my most faithful companion." As a child, drawing was Raffael's favorite activity, and he spent many hours drawing at home. He liked to do things that allowed him to be alone with nature, like ice-skating, roller-skating, and walking. Today, Raffael often creates his radiant watercolors on more than one piece of paper or multi-paneled pieces. Sometimes he creates screens with five or more panels, and sometimes he makes diptychs of two painted panels hinged together. Raffael is well known for large-scale watercolor or acrylic paintings of nature and the use of many different colors in a single composition. He may use as many as 20 to 30 shades of blue in one painting!

Mega-Shiny Diptych

Create a super-size painting on two joined sheets of paper using a homemade paint recipe for shiny, translucent paint. By hinging the two sheets together, the painting will appear as one superb mega-painting called a diptych.

Materials

two large sheets of white paper
clear tape
Shiny Glue-Paint (see below)

paintbrushes
large, flat workspace (floor, table, wall)
pushpins

Shiny Glue-Paint Recipe

Pour or squeeze white glue into paper cups, one for each color of paint chosen.
Add different colors of liquid tempera paint to each cup.
Add a few drops of liquid dishwashing detergent to each cup to help smooth the paint and make it adhere better to paper.
Stir well.

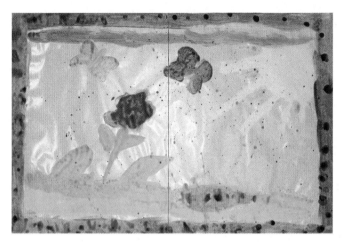

Shiny Glue Garden Diptych, by Irina Ammosova, 8

Process

❶ Experiment with the style of Raffael, mixing different shades of the same color when making the Shiny Glue Paint. For example, mix several cups of blues (navy, sky, robin's egg, periwinkle), or several cups of reds (pink, magenta, fire engine, cherry). Test the paint on white paper to see if it appears shiny, radiant, and translucent. More paint or glue may be added to adjust colors.

❷ To create a diptych, simply run a long piece of tape on the seam joining the two sheets of paper, and then turn the sheets over so the tape is on the back. The two sheets will form one large sheet with the taped hinge on the back.

❸ Raffael paints subjects of nature, including images of water, trees, flowers, and birds. He often paints a frame around the main subject. With the shiny paint and choice of paintbrushes, fill the large joined sheets of paper with colorful images of nature from imagination. Fill the entire paper with color, leaving an unpainted 2- to 3-inch border or frame.

❹ Next, paint the wide border with specks and dots of paints, if desired, or leave completely untouched.

❺ Allow the painting to dry until shiny and clear. Secure for display with pushpins on a large, open wall.

Flowers Diptych with Dotted Frame, by Madeline VandeHoef, 8

Faith Ringgold

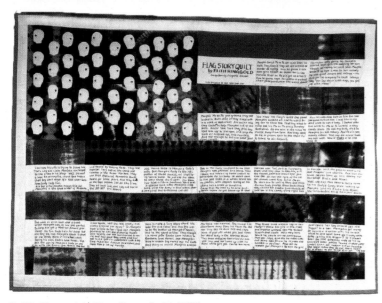

Faith Ringgold | *Flag Story Quilt*, 1985
Cotton canvas, dyed, pieced, 1448 × 1982 cm, Spencer Museum of Art, Peter T. Bohan Art Aquisition Fund, 1991.40 © Faith Ringgold 1985

October 8, 1930–
Fiber Artist, Narrative

Faith Ringgold [REENG gohld] was born in Harlem in New York City as the youngest of three children. She often had to stay home from school because she had severe asthma. Her mother helped her with her homework and showed her how to work with crayons, fabrics, and sewing. Her father also helped, teaching her to read and giving her a paint easel. When Ringgold grew up, she became an art teacher and professor of art at the University of California, San Diego. When her mother died, Ringgold began making quilts as a tribute. Faith Ringgold is best known for creating story quilts—art that combines painting and quilted fabric as a way of telling stories about her people and heritage. Faith Ringgold and fabric artist Grace Matthews were commissioned to design and construct a special story quilt inspired by New York City children who had created images for the book, *What Will You Do for Peace?* After the tragic events of September 11, 2001, these young peace quilt artists were brought together by the InterRelations Collaborative to transfer their artwork from the peace book to the peace quilt. Read about the journey of the peace quilt at www.inter-relations.org.

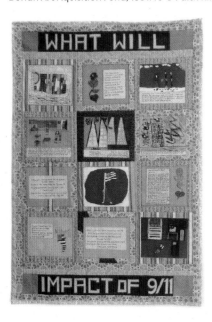  

Faith Ringgold and Grace Matthews, design and construction, in collaboration with New York City children and youth participating in IRC's 9/11 PeaceMaking Initiative | *9/11 Peace Story Quilt*
Fabric and paint, 72 × 50 in © 2006 InterRelations Collaborative, Inc. Commissioned by the InterRelations Collaborative, Inc., Funded by The Andrew W. Mellon Foundation and The United Way of New York City

Wishing Quilt

There are many ways to make a quilt! In this basic quilt activity, use fabric crayons to draw an important wish on a white piece of paper. Iron-transfer the drawing to a flat, white twin sheet. To complete the quilt, an adult can sew the decorated sheet to a quilt backing. Kids can help sew too! Add decorating ideas with embroidery, sewing trims, buttons, or hand lettering with permanent markers.

Twin Sheet Quilt with Iron-On Designs

Materials

one twin flat white
   bedsheet
yardstick
permanent marker
white paper
fabric crayons
iron
ironing board
large clean rag
clean sheets of
   newsprint
sewing supplies:
   scissors, straight
   pins, sewing
   machine,
   thread
decorating tools:
   permanent
   markers,
   embroidery
   thread and
   needle, sewing
   trims, buttons,
   yarn and large
   needle
fabric backing

Process

Transferring Wish Drawings

❶ An adult can mark off a section for each wish square on the twin sheet using the permanent marker and yardstick. A twin sheet should measure out to hold about twenty 12-inch squares, 4 squares across by 5 squares down.

❷ Each young artist can draw an important wish on white paper with fabric crayons. Draw with strong and colorful strokes. The colors may look a little dull on the paper, but will transfer to the fabric in very bright permanent color.

❸ With adult help, iron-transfer each drawing onto a section of the white sheet. Follow the directions on the fabric crayon box, usually covering the ironing board with clean newsprint or a clean rag, then the sheet, next the drawing face down, and then another rag or newsprint. The iron should be set warm without steam. Press the iron firmly without wiggling. Move the press to the entire drawing. Then remove the materials to see the transfer on the white square. It will be bright and clear!

❹ Each section can be further decorated with sewing trims, buttons, or embroidery. Hand-lettered words can be added with permanent marker, but be careful, there's no erasing permanent marker!

Constructing the Basic Quilt

Note: Many children are capable of working with a sewing machine with adult help.

❶ Join the sheet to the puffy backing: Spread the backing face up on the workspace or floor. Position the sheet with iron-on designs face down on the backing, centering, and matching edges and corners. Pin in place.

❷ Machine-sew the backing to the sheet, sewing three sides in a long running stitch (two long sides and the top short side). Sew the fourth side, but leave it partway open in the middle. Remove the pins. Turn the quilt right side out by pulling it through the opening.

❸ Turn in the open area of the seam and sew it down. If desired, top-stitch about 1 inch in from the edge along all four sides. This completes the basic sheet quilt.

❹ To stabilize the double layers of the quilt, sew short yarn pieces (6 inches or so) through the corner of each section. Tie the yarn in a knot and snip off extra yarn. You may also sew long running lines between sections, as in the photo.

Jim Dine

June 16, 1935–
Pop Art painter, sculptor

Jim Dine [dyn] was born in Cincinnati, Ohio, and grew up in the Midwest. Dine became an extremely versatile artist. In just four decades, he has produced more than 3,000 paintings, sculptures, drawings, and prints, as well as performance works, stage and book designs, poetry, and even music. Dine is known for repeating images over and over in his art, reinventing them in a variety of ways each time. He uses images that feel personal and familiar and part of people's lives, like the hands, bathrobe, tools, and his most recognized symbol, the heart. Dine's work is part of the Pop Art movement, along with other Pop artists (Lichtenstein p. 70, Warhol p. 67, and Thiebaud p. 68). Jim Dine's art can be see at www.artnet.com.

Heart Works

Divide drawing paper into sections. Trace or draw a heart into each space in a repeating pattern. Decorate each heart and the background of each section with different designs or colors using a choice of techniques with pastels, markers, chalks, or crayons.

Materials

drawing paper, any size
coloring materials: oil
    pastels, pastel chalks,
    crayons, markers
scissors (optional)

sheet of colored paper
    for a mat or frame
    (optional)
tape, stapler, glue (optional)

Process

❶ Section the drawing paper into squares. Four is a good number for beginners, and eight works especially well, but any number is fine. Fold the paper and crease well to create sections. Then unfold and flatten the paper on the workspace.

❷ Draw a heart freehand in each section, filling each space. Color and decorate each heart with a different color and design. Don't forget to design and color the background of the heart too. Make patterns, plaids, solids, dots, wiggles, cross-hatching, and any imaginable designs. See "More Color Techniques" for ideas.

❸ When done, the drawing paper can be glued, taped, or stapled to a larger sheet of colored paper to make a simple mat or frame.

Heart Work, by Kendra Johnson, grade 3
Courtesy of April Barlett, Art Teacher, Arthur Ashe Elementary School, Richmond, Virginia

More Color Techniques

- Markers Over: Color over some of the crayoned hearts with markers (not permanent). The water-based color will resist the wax in the crayon. Some artists like to rub the marker color with a tissue to further blur and blend.
- Chalk Blend: Blend in pastels or chalk colors with tissues or fingers.

Speedy Stencil Tracing

Draw one heart on heavier paper, cut it out with scissors, and trace this heart stencil in each section. Use both parts of the shapes—positive and negative!

A Big Heart, by
Morgan Marshall, 6

Frank Philip Stella

May 12, 1936–
Abstract, Minimalist painter

Frank Philip Stella [STEL-uh], born in Malden, Massachusetts, is an American painter and printmaker. He was influenced by Abstract Expressionists like Jackson Pollock (see p. 56). When Stella moved to New York City and began painting in 1950, he was drawn toward "flatter" surface art like Jasper Johns's target paintings (p. 66). Stella said that a picture was "a flat surface with paint on it, nothing more." Though a master of Minimalist and Abstract styles, Stella is particularly well known for painting grids and mazes in an array of lines, shapes, and geometric patterns. Stella worked with copper and aluminum paint in his first mazes. He also produced paintings on shaped canvases (not the usual rectangular or square), often using letter shapes like the L, N, U, or T. Stella lives in New York, and his works can be viewed at numerous galleries and art museums. Stella said, "When I'm painting the picture, I'm really painting a picture. To me, the thrill . . . of the thing is the actual painting."

Frank Stella | *Sinjerli Variation IV*, 1968
Acrylic on canvas, 120 in diameter, Wadsworth Atheneum Museum of Art, Hartford, Connecticut. The Ella Gallup Sumner and Mary Catlin Sumner Collection Fund, and partial gift of Mr. and Mrs. Burton Tremaine, Sr., 1982.157 Image © Wadsworth Atheneum Museum of Art, Art © 2008 Frank Stella/ Artists Rights Society (ARS), New York

Concentric Paint

Design a concentric circle artwork with an array of color. Try metallic paint. A concentric design is like a target, where lines and shapes share the same center. As with most modern art, the circles can be any size and design.

Materials

white posterboard or large drawing
     paper
pencil
drawing tools: crayons, colored
     pencils, markers, tempera paints,
     metallic paints
paintbrushes
metallic pens

Process

❶ Lightly sketch a circular shape in the center of the poster-board. The circle can be perfectly round or may be shaped in an interesting way. This will be the center of the concentric design. The rest of the design will radiate outward from this.

❷ A little way from the edge of the first circle, draw another line that completely circles the first. It can be perfectly measured, or more surprising in its shape, as long as it completely circles the first. Draw a third line that circles the second, and so on, until the posterboard is filled to the edge with concentric circles. Concentric means the circles start from the center and circle one another outward, like an artistic target.

❸ Paint or color the spaces between the lines with an array of colors. Changing colors within one space can add interest.

❹ Consider using metallic paints to fill in concentric areas or to high-light lines or shapes in any way. If metallic paint is not available, metallic marking pens from a craft or office store can be used to trace lines or fill in smaller areas.

Crayon Target, Art by a child, age 4, using full arm movements on a large sheet of paper taped to the wall.

97

Alan Magee

Alan Magee | *Countermeasure*, 2004
Acrylic on canvas, 50 × 75 in, Courtesy of the artist
© 2004 Alan Magee

Alan Magee working, Courtesy of the artist,
Photography © 2007 Monika Magee

May 26, 1947–
Realist painter

Alan Magee [muh GEE] was born in Newtown, Pennsylvania. He is a Realist, sometimes called a Representational painter, as well as a sculptor, printmaker, and photographer. Magee is best known for his large-scale acrylic paintings of stones and found objects—images that are highly realistic and visually astounding. When asked if he looks at real stones or pictures of stones for inspiration, Magee replied, "I spend a lot of time at one particular beach in Maine. I don't think it's possible to paint anything convincingly unless you've looked at it carefully, so I return to those stones again and again to get to know them better. I make the paintings in my studio. In the past I worked from photographs I'd taken at the beach, but in recent years I've worked from arrangements of stones that I make in the studio." Magee works long days—beginning early and often continuing to paint into the evening hours. He says that creative work is a pleasure, not a chore. He loved to draw when he was a child and enjoyed looking closely at things. Earlier in his artistic career, Magee illustrated covers for books, winning a National Book Award in 1982. His illustrations and paintings have received numerous honors. Alan Magee lives and works in Maine, a place that is a great source of inspiration for his art.

Rock On

Get to know stones and rocks! Find loose stones in nature and arrange or stack them creatively. Take a picture to capture the work for viewing long after the arrangement is gone. Be sure to return the pieces to their original places or positions (stacked rocks could fall and hurt small creatures in the wild).

Materials

collected natural materials: stones, rocks, pebbles, gravel, leaves, twigs, bark, pinecones
base or background for sculpture: sand, dirt, lawn, sidewalk, playground
stick for drawing in the sand or dirt
camera
tape or glue (optional)
posterboard (optional)

Process

❶ Working outdoors, collect stones or rocks or other materials from nature. Assemble them in one area.

❷ Stack or place the items in a design or temporary sculpture. Add other natural bits and pieces to decorate the art further, if desired.

❸ To add interest, draw around the arrangement in the sand or dirt with a stick. As an additional idea, arrange leaves or sand in a design or pattern around the arrangement.

❹ When satisfied with the art, take pictures from different angles. When they are printed, look them over to see how the arrangement looks from each view. Tape or glue the photos on posterboard, if desired.

❺ To maintain the natural environment for bugs and small animals, try to return the area to its natural state.

Rock Flower, MaryAnn Kohl

River Beach in Northwest Washington, MaryAnn Kohl

Chuck Close

Chuck Close painting a self-portrait in his studio.
Photograph by Michael Marfione, PaceWildenstein, New York
Image from Walker Art Center, Minneapolis, Minnesota, © Chuck Close

July 5, 1940–
Photorealist painter

Chuck Close [klohs] grew up in the small town of Monroe, Washington, near Seattle. Though school was difficult for Close because his learning disabilities made it hard for him to study, he discovered his best subject in college in Tacoma, Washington. Art became his life's work! Close is best known for giant portraits—paintings of faces on huge canvas 8 to 12 feet high. Over the years, he moved from super-detailed realism to a completely unique painting style based on photographs created with a grid of colorful ovals and squares. The grid breaks the image down into smaller sections that he paints by hand. He applies one careful stroke after another in multicolors, or multi-grays. In 1988, when he already was a successful artist, Close was paralyzed by a rare illness. With much time and hard work, his condition has improved and he now paints from his wheelchair with a special arm brace that allows him to work. His strength and ability to adapt and explore different techniques have allowed Chuck Close to invent a new style of art and expand the definition of what a truly great American artist can be. He said, "I am going for a level of perfection that is only mine. Most of the pleasure is in getting the last little piece perfect." See Chuck Close's art at www.pacegallery.com/artists/80/chuck-close.

Grid Banana, by Joy Pastor, 12

Color Grid

To experiment with creating a color grid, fold a square of white drawing paper in half, and then in half again several times to form squares. Flatten the paper and fill in each square with colorful blobs, targets, X's, solids, or even combine a few squares to make one larger shape. This grid will not form a picture of an object, but it will be an exciting artistic experiment in grid design.

Materials

drawing paper
coloring or painting supplies: tempera paint and brushes, pastels, markers, crayons, oil pastels, colored pencils, chalk

Process

❶ To make a grid, fold a square of paper in half, and then in half again, until the whole square is scored with smaller squares. From a sheet of paper about 6-inches wide with 4 squares across and 4 down, each square will be about 1½ inches in size. Using a larger square produces larger spaces when folded, and a smaller square produces smaller folded spaces.

❷ Open and then flatten the folded paper on the workspace.

❸ Experiment with filling in each square with color and design. Here are some shapes and suggestions:

solid box	teardrop	triangle	target
blob	circle	ring	concentric
X mark	diamond	dot	

❹ Let a satisfying feeling of design and color guide how the squares are filled.

Chuck Close Super Challenge

Look at a photograph of a piece of fruit, or look closely at a real piece of fruit, such as an apple or a banana. Stare at it, and notice all the colors and shapes and designs on the surface of the fruit. The apple will not be just solid red or green, and the banana will not be just yellow. Look carefully. Next, draw the outline of the piece of fruit on grid paper. Then fill in the squares of the grid within the lines of the fruit showing the fruit with detailed design and color.

Grid with Melted Copper Crayon,
Cristina Hernandez, 8

Seven by Seven Color Grid,
Maddison Fox, 8

Jewell Praying Wolf James

The Liberty and Freedom totem poles with the Sovereignty cross-bar. Photograph © Rudi Williams, US Department of Defense, American Forces Press Service

Sanded Wood Spirits

Carving weathered wood is like looking at clouds for images that are hidden. Study the piece of wood for its hidden image, then with sanding tools, remove enough wood to make the image visible. Very young artists should first explore carving or whittling a bar of soap with a plastic knife. More experienced carvers can use formal carving tools like knives, chisels, gouges, and chip carvers.

Materials

weathered wood or driftwood piece
newspaper
permanent markers (optional)
paints and brushes (optional)
sanding and tool supplies: small dowels,
   flat sticks, sandpaper, glue, scissors

February 2, 1953–
Wood Carver, Traditional native

Jewell Praying Wolf James [jaymz], native name tse-Sealth, is a descendent of Chief Seattle. He was born on the Lummi Indian Reservation in western Washington, where he has lived his entire life. James is a Master Carver of the House of Tears, a group who wanted to raise awareness of the need for healing within tribes, among races, and among nations. James and the House of Tears are best known for carving the Lummi Healing Pole, which was carried to the Sterling Forest north of New York City to commemorate the victims of the September 11, 2001, tragedy. The pole received healing blessings from many tribes as it made its way across the United States. Of his childhood, Jewell James says, "As a grade-school child, I always liked drawing. I think most kids like the feeling it gives them because something in the right brain is activated. In the third grade, I really loved the way I drew blue jays and robins. I never shared them with anyone. It was like my secret way of expressing something inside that needed expressing." The House of Tears originally consisted of James, his brother Dale, Kenny Cooper, and Vern Johnson. Of the original House of Tears, James is the only one still living.

Process

❶ Make sandpaper tools by gluing sandpaper over the end and halfway down a small dowel. Any technique of wrapping and gluing the sandpaper is fine. The dowel will be used to rub away wood, using both the point of the dowel and the sides. Round sticks and flat sticks act differently, so make both. Note: Some artists like to wrap a piece of sandpaper around the head of a screwdriver, held in place with the carving hand, to accomplish serious sanding.

❷ Study the weathered wood piece. Begin to carve the wood by removing sharp edges and smoothing it with a sanding tool. Use various points and sides of the sandpaper tools to remove more wood, revealing the hidden image for others to see. This can take some time.

Quinn VanderHoef, 9, sands a piece of driftwood

❸ As an optional idea, highlight or color parts of the wood to make it more visible. Traditional Coast Salish colors would be black, red, and white. Jewell James often leaves his carvings uncolored.

Pepón Osorio

June 10, 1955–
Installation sculptor

Pepón Osorio [oh-SOHR-ee-oh] was born Benjamin Osorio Encarnación in Puerto Rico. He later moved to the South Bronx in New York City, where he studied sociology, ultimately building a career helping protect Latino American children from abuse. He continues to be deeply attached to his South Bronx community as his center of inspiration and drive. Osorio sees himself as an interpreter who brings subjects from his community to those on the outside. He is best known for his large installations, sculptures that are assemblages of found objects—plastic toys, baubles, trinkets, and souvenirs. These *chucherías* used in his artworks are symbols of feelings, experiences, and memories. Osorio's works are flashy and great favorites of children, although there is often a deeper, more serious message hidden in his seemingly humorous art. Of one of his artworks, Osario says he wanted to "collect an entire community's events and feelings in one place."

Pepón Osorio | *La Bicicleta*, 1985
© Pepón Osorio 2008, used by permission of Ronald Feldman Fine Arts, New York

Trinket Sculpture

Decorate an object with a collection of collage materials that expresses a theme or message. Collecting materials will be half the fun. An old bicycle is especially entertaining as the main object. A sculpture of this size is a good group project but can just as well be created by an individual or partners with time and room to create.

Materials

large object to decorate as permanent art: bicycle, chair, lamp, wagon, picture frame, skateboard
items for decorating: buttons, novelty pins, silk flowers or leaves, toy building pieces, party favors, plastic flowers or leaves, fabric scraps, paper scraps, mardi gras beads, paper umbrellas, photographs, playing cards, costume jewelry, stamps, toy flags, wood scraps, ribbons, streamers, stickers, small animal figures, dolls, cars, toy fruits or vegetables
assembling supplies: glue (white, tacky, hot glue), tape (masking, duct, packing), thread, string, yarn, wire, rubber bands, stapler, scissors

Process

❶ Set up the main object to be decorated in an area with plenty of room for creating. A theme or message should be chosen to be expressed through the assemblage. Some ideas are:
- express a happy event such as a birthday or holiday
- relate the story of a family or group and all their interests
- show a simple theme based on a word such as Happy, Silly, Sports, or Spring.
Whatever the theme or message is, it should come through loud and strong based on which items are chosen and attached to the main object.

❷ Spread or sort the trinkets and decorations in muffin tins, boxes, or on a table. Think about what to attach, and then jump in! Cover the large object with the items that express the theme best. Some adult help might be needed with glue, but most things can be attached easily. Then, dry as needed.

❸ Part of creating a large assemblage is displaying it, which is called an "installation." Install it on a wall, from a ceiling, or set it up in an area where it can be viewed from all four sides.

Beverly Buchanan

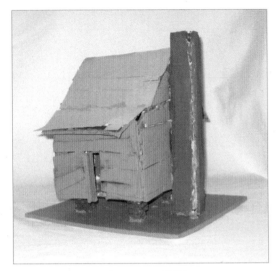

Beverly Buchanan | *Survivor*, 2007
Multimedia sculpture, 9½ H × 9½ W × 9¼ L in, Courtesy of the artist, © Beverly Buchanan 2007. All rights reserved.

October 8, 1940–July 4, 2015
Regionalist, Folk sculptor and artist

Beverly Buchanan [byoo-KAN-uhn] was an African American artist noted for art-works that explore the Southern architecture that was so much a part of her child-hood. Buchanan grew up in Orangeburg, South Carolina, where she and her agri-cultural scientist father traveled throughout the state. She saw the poor people and their dwellings up close. The shacks she saw were built by hand out of whatever was on hand: bits of wood, metal, tar paper, and scrap. When she grew up, Buchanan followed her interest in science and medicine as a career and attended medical school, but she soon focused on her art, expressing the images, stories, and architecture of her childhood. Beverly Buchanan is best known for showing the image of "the shack"—the small cabin-like shelter seen in the fields and along the back roads of the South. Buchanan's shacks range from bright and cheerful to eerie and white. She often exhibited her photo-graphs alongside her drawings and sculptures. Buchanan said the shacks she created are "memorials to people and places" of her rural South.

Island Beach Retreat, by Sarah, 12,
Wesley, 10, and Morgan Van Slyke, 12

Shack Sculpture

On a cardboard base, construct a building or home with col-lected scrap materials. Use glue, tape, nails, string, or other materials to bind the structure together. Construct an imagi-nary model, or an actual house or cabin remembered, lived in, or photographed along the way.

Materials

cardboard base, 6-inches square or larger
scrap materials: cardboard, mat board, posterboard, scrap paper, sticks or twigs, aluminum foil, craft sticks, wood scraps, wire, playing cards, plastic wrap

building tools: pliers, scissors, duct tape yarn, string, rope
with adult assistance: wire cutter, hack saw, hammer, nails, glue gun
paint and paintbrush

Process

❶ Spread out the selection of scraps and materials on the workspace. Arrange tools within reach.
❷ To begin, build the general frame of the structure. Pull together some sticks or cardboard strips for building walls for the shack using the card-board base as the floor. A strong basic frame for the structure will enable all other elements to be added.
❸ Add windows, roof, walls, and other unique details. Some possibilities include a chimney, door (knob, hinges, window), shingles, siding, porch, potted plants, or steps.
❹ If necessary, tape or tie the structure together to hold until glue dries. Then paint, if desired.
❺ Display the completed structure with a photograph of the actual build-ing, if one was taken. The structure could also be displayed with a drawing or plan of the sculpture. Otherwise, display the structure independently.

Maya Lin

October 5, 1959–
Architect

Maya Lin [lin] was born in Ohio to parents who immigrated to America from China. Both her mother and father were university professors: her mother, a poet and writer; her father, a ceramics artist. Lin studied to be an architect at Yale University. At Yale she entered and won a competition for designing the Vietnam Veterans Memorial. Maya Lin's famous tribute to American soldiers who died during the war in Vietnam is located in a park in Washington, DC. The long, V-shaped wall of black stone seems to rise out of the earth. The face of the wall is carved with more than 58,000 names of soldiers who died. It is the most visited monument in the US capital. Lin has created many memorials since her famous Vietnam Veterans Memorial was completed in 1982. Lin's monuments use architecture, sculpture, and the area's landscape to create a special environment that will encourage visitors to pause and to think.

Maya Lin | The Vietnam Memorial, 1982.
Photograph © A. Lee Bennett Jr./www.ATPM.com

Memorial Plaque

A memorial is a way to remember someone or something important. Create a memorial plaque using Plaster of Paris embellished with acrylic paint.

Materials

sketch paper
pencil
black crayon
foam grocery tray
Plaster of Paris
plastic cup and craft stick
large nail
masking tape
spray bottle filled with water
acrylic paints in gold, tan, and gray
gloss hobby coating and brush (optional)

Process

1. Think of someone to honor with a memorial artwork: a family member, beloved pet, or hero.
2. First trace around the grocery tray on paper. Then draw the memorial art to fit in the tracing. Use a few words and a simple symbolic illustration (sunshine, candle flame, rose, dove, etc.). Then turn the paper over and color over the back of the design heavily with black crayon to ready it for transfer.
3. In the plastic cup, mix 1 cup Plaster of Paris and some water with a stick to a thick milkshake consistency. Pour the plaster into the grocery tray and tap gently to settle and smooth the surface. (See plaster safety note.)
4. After the plaster has hardened for an hour, gently remove the plaque from the tray. To transfer the design, hold the sketch face up on top of the plaster. Trace over the lines with a pencil. Faint crayon marks will transfer to the plaster beneath.
5. Wrap the point of a nail with masking tape, and gently scratch into the plaster. Scrape the nail point along transferred crayon lines. Be careful not to crack the plaster. Lightly spray the plaster with water to dampen during this engraving process to prevent dust.
6. When carving is complete, use a soft cloth or paper towel to rub acrylic paint onto the plaque. Start with light colors, then rub darker colors over the light. The dark paint will sink into the carved lines. Dabs and splatters will give the plaster a "stone" appearance. Let the plaque dry for several days.
7. A final optional coat of clear hobby coating gives a shiny finish. The memorial plaque works well as an indoor display. If placed outdoors, the plaque will gradually weather and crumble away.

Plaster Safety Note

Plaster of Paris should be handled and mixed in its powder form by adults, preventing children from accidentally breathing dust. Never wash Plaster of Paris down the drain as it may cause a serious clog.

Bev Doolittle

Bev Doolittle | *Missed*, 1985
Watercolor, 17 × 13 in, Courtesy of the artist and
The Greenwich Workshop © 2007. All rights reserved.

February 10, 1947–
Concept painter

Bev Doolittle [DOO-lit-uhl] was born and raised in California and considers herself a visual storyteller, using camouflage as a technique to visually slow how people look at her work. She wants people to think when they look at her paintings. "Many people call me a camouflage artist, but . . . I prefer to think of myself as a concept painter. I am an artist who uses camouflage to get my story across, to slow the viewing process so they can discover it for themselves. My meaning and message are never hidden." In 1968, Bev Doolittle graduated from the Art Center College of Design in Los Angeles where she met and then married her husband. The Doolittles prefer being close to nature and traveling, rather than living in a big city. Bev Doolittle's subject matter comes from the outdoors and the Western wilderness. Look carefully at Bev Doolittle's artworks on this page and discover the message that she says is "never hidden."

Bev Doolittle | *Two Indian Horses*, 1985
Watercolor, 48 × 7¾ in, Courtesy of the artist and
The Greenwich Workshop © 2007. All rights reserved.

Camouflage Mixed Media

Draw and construct a camouflage artwork using masking tape as the secret component that creates a white birch forest. Hand drawn animals hide within.

Materials

large white drawing paper

painter's tape

pencil

crayons or oil pastels

Process

❶ To begin, arrange the white drawing paper horizontally (the long way) on the table.

❷ To create a birch tree forest, stretch pieces of painter's tape vertically up and down across the paper, like a fence, with spaces between. Each piece of tape will eventually become a birch tree. Five to ten trees should be about right, but fewer is fine. Leaving spaces between the trees will offer more room for drawing.

❸ Draw any subject on the paper that might be found in a birch forest, like children hiking, a grazing deer, or a wolf peering out of the trees. Draw right over the masking tape as if it were not there at all.

❹ Next color the drawing with clear and strong colors. Color right over the masking tape birch forest. With a pencil, lightly sketch in other camouflage subjects in the rest of the paper, such as forest birds, owls, rabbits, or squirrels. Lightly color these camouflage subjects so they are visible, but not bright, bold, or highly colored.

❺ Now for the best part! Carefully peel the masking tape from the paper. Go slowly. Some of the sketches and drawings will be removed with the tape, but don't worry—it's part of the camouflage fun! When all the tape pieces are peeled, add little stripes and markings to make each clean peeled area look like birch bark. Add leaves or other decorative tree details. Use color wherever desired.

❻ The trees will camouflage the animal subjects, as if they are hidden in the forest. Viewers will have to look carefully to see the hidden animals, just like in the artworks of Bev Doolittle.

Purple Birds in Birch Trees,
by Francesca Martinelli, 6

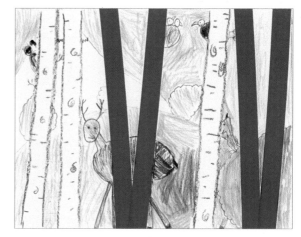

Deer in the Doolittle Forest, by Tore Olson, 10
(in proces of removing tape)

Dale Chihuly

Dale Chihuly | *Niijima Floats*, 2005
Fairchild Tropical Botanic Garden, Coral Gables, Florida, Photo by Terry Rishel, © Dale Chihuly 2005

September 20, 1941–
Glass artist, Installation

Dale Patrick Chihuly [chi HOO lee] was born the second of two children in his family in Tacoma, Washington. He says about glass: "I was first taken with glass as a little kid walking along the beach, picking up bits of glass and shells. Perhaps it was a bottle, broken on a rock into a hundred pieces, which was then dispersed on the beach for a hundred different kids to find." Chihuly's father was a meat cutter. His mother, a very important influence in his life, was a homemaker. When he went to college, Chihuly majored in interior design partly because he had enjoyed decorating a basement room for her. When he graduated, Chihuly "became obsessed with glass" and went on to study glassblowing in graduate school. In 1971, Chihuly cofounded the Pilchuck School in Stanwood, Washington, where his blown-glass sculptures and assemblages grew in fame, size, color, and design. Chihuly now operates a team approach at his Boathouse glassblowing hotshop and studio in Seattle. "It inspires me to be working with a group of people on an idea. It's the way things happen for me." He describes himself saying, "I call myself an artist for lack of a better word. I'm an artist, a designer, a craftsman, interior designer, half-architect. There's no one name that fits me very well." Children particularly enjoy Chihuly's exciting outdoor installations like his floating glass spheres, *Niijima Floats* (referring to the floats Japanese fishermen tied to their nets in the past), the largest blown-glass spheres ever made. Thanks to Dale Chihuly, glassmaking has become a popular and highly recognized form of fine art in America.

Pool Spheres

Create a water-and-spheres installation starting with a flat container filled with water as the base of the sculpture. Next, assemble greenery and natural materials, and finish with colorful floating spheres arranged within the tiny pool in the style of Chihuly's *Niijima Floats*.

Floating Spheres in My Yard, by Royce Zahn, 5

Materials

small water container: serving bowl, pie pan, casserole dish, plastic tub

natural landscape materials: pebbles, gravel, rocks, stones, leaves, blossoms (natural, plastic, or silk), moss, small branches with leaves

white Ping-Pong balls

permanent markers in assorted colors and sizes

water

apron or smock

newspapers

Process

❶ Select a place to build the mini installation, a table or counter where others can view and enjoy the completed artwork. Set the bowl or dish on a flat area where splashes of water will not harm the surface beneath. Gather all the materials from the list that will be needed.

❷ Before filling the dish with water, line the bottom of the "pool" in a decorative way with natural materials such as rocks, gravel, sand, and/or pebbles. This will take a while to do. Moss can be used to line the dish or can be added later.

❸ Gently fill the container with several inches of water, being careful not to disturb the lining of rocks and sand. Next, add greenery, either floating free or held in place with rocks. The idea is to make the little pool look natural.

❹ Add color and design to the Ping-Pong balls with permanent marker pens. Permanent pens can stain fingers and clothes, so work on newspapers and wear a paint smock or apron.

❺ Float the colored balls on the water. Arrange as many floating balls as desired, watching for a color and shape that is satisfying. Enjoy how the air currents cause the sculpture to change. Invite others to view the Pool Spheres.

Outdoor Pool Installation

A small wading pool filled with water creates an exciting, challenging, and larger-scale outdoor installation. Use balloons or toy balls of all kinds for the spheres, and employ plenty of natural landscaping to decorate.

Ping-Pong Winter Garden, by Amy Barber, 6

Kara Walker

Kara Walker | *Untitled*, 1998
Cut paper and wax adhesive on wall, 80 × 55 in, Courtesy of
Sikkema Jenkins & Co. All rights reserved

November 26, 1969–
Silhouette artist, Installation

Kara Walker [WAHL-kur] was born in Stockton, California. When Kara was 13, she, her parents, and her two siblings moved to Atlanta so her artist father, Larry Walker, could begin teaching art at Georgia State University. Walker showed talent at a young age and says, "One of my earliest memories involves sitting on my dad's lap in his studio in the garage of our house and watching him draw. I remember thinking, 'I want to do that, too,' and I pretty much decided then and there at age two or three that I was an artist just like Dad." When she grew up, Kara Walker became known for her room-sized panoramic cut-paper silhouettes, most often black figures against a white wall, expressing racial messages and powerful themes of slavery in history. Sometimes Walker adds colored lights from projectors to cast shadows or highlight scenes. Many of Walker's silhouettes will be enjoyed by children. However, Walker's art can be intense or graphic, so adults should preview Internet searches before children are invited to view. Walker currently lives in New York, where she is a professor of visual arts at Columbia University and the mother of a young daughter who, Walker says, like other small viewers, responds to the scale of her large works.

Video stills from Kara Walker | *8 Possible Beginnings or:*
The Creation of African-America, a Moving Picture
B&W video, 15:57 minutes, Video still courtesy of
Sikkema Jenkins & Co. All rights reserved.

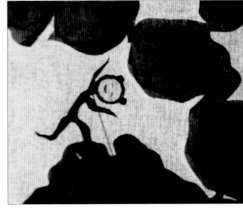 

Freehand Silhouettes

Cut silhouettes from colored paper freehand, which means cutting without drawing the shapes first. Assemble a group of silhouettes to make a scene on a wall.

Materials

construction paper, any color
scissors
black construction paper
tape
light source (optional): flashlight, overhead
  projector, window

Process

❶ To warm up and practice cutting a freehand silhouette, cut a simple shape from a scrap of colored construction paper. Then try a few more to get the idea. These shapes are called silhouettes. They are like shadows without all the details that can be seen in the light.

❷ Think of a shape, animal, object, person, or design. Without drawing first, cut the silhouette shape freehand directly from the black construction paper. Use good scissors so the cut designs are crisp.

❸ Cut more silhouettes, perhaps creating a scene of several things that go together in some way. Here are some ideas:
  • two cats playing with a ball of string
  • a mother and father and child walking or hugging
  • a jungle animal with trees and plants
  • a person jumping rope or shooting a basketball
  • flowers in a vase or growing in a garden
  • houses and buildings lining a street (windows can be cut out)

Silhouette Leaves in Color

Sailboat

Snake in the Grass

Halloween Octopus

Lime Tulip and Lemon Bunny

Silhouettes by Morgan Van Slyke, 12 and Dianna Barker, 7

❹ Tape the silhouettes to a wall or large piece of paper. Some artists will wish to create a scene, and others will prefer to cut and display a variety of unrelated silhouettes.

Shadows and Light

  • Shine a flashlight or other bright light on the silhouette wall in a darkened room.
  • Project construction paper silhouettes on an overhead projector, shining them on the wall.
  • Place silhouettes cut from thin, colorful art tissue on a window.

Janet Fish

Janet Fish, *A.M.*, 1994

Screenprint on Rives BFK paper ® Janet Fish 1994, Photo courtesy of
www.StewartStewart.com, Art © Janet Fish/Licensed by VAGA, New York, NY

Janet Fish working on her screenprint *A.M.*

Photograph © www.StewartStewart.com 1994, Art
© Janet Fish/Licensed by VAGA, New York, NY

May 18, 1938–
Realist painter

Janet Fish was born in Boston and raised in Bermuda, a bright and sunny British territory in the North Atlantic Ocean. As a child, Janet liked picking up old bottles from the beach, just like her father liked to do, as well as saving other intriguing items that washed ashore. Her family's interest and talent in art must have been an inspiration to her. Her grandfather was a famous American Impressionist painter, her uncle was a woodcarver, and her mother was a sculptor and potter. With art such an important part of her family life, it seems natural that Fish went on to study art as she grew up, and that she continued on into adulthood with a masterful career in art. Fish thinks of herself as a "painterly realist," interested in light, atmosphere, motion, and saturated color. She is best known for still life paintings that include clear glass jars, vases, and dishes. She arranges things on colorful tabletops and fills the dishes with fruits and flowers. Her oil paintings, pastels, and watercolors show light sparkling from crystal glass surfaces and intriguing reflections in the shiny glass. She often paints objects showing through the glass, sometimes through many different layers. Fish says, "I feel as though I haven't seen an object until I actually start painting it." Janet Fish's paintings are masterpieces of light and color.

Still Life with Glass

A still life is a painting of objects arranged in a group. With watercolors, paint a still life of an arrangement set on a patterned tablecloth, and a clear glass container with a flower in it. For added shine and fun, cover the glass area of the painting with clear plastic wrap cut and glued to fit.

Materials

tablecloth with colored pattern	white watercolor paper or sheet of drawing paper
clear glass or plastic container, such as a jar or vase	watercolor paints and water
water	paintbrush
still life arrangement items to fit container	clear plastic wrap
pencil and eraser	marker
scrap drawing paper	scissors
	white glue

Process

❶ Crumple a tablecloth on a work area so it has folds. Set the glass container on top of the cloth. Fill it with water. Place your still life item in the container. A flower or branch—or even a fish!—are good options.

❷ Draw the still life lightly with pencil on a practice sheet of paper. When satisfied, draw it on the watercolor paper, drawing lightly and large.

❸ Paint the pencil drawing with watercolors. Watery blues and greens are good for the clear glass. Leave the areas that will be bright or white unpainted.

Janet the Fish, by Ella Zahn, 9

Flowers by the Window, by Irina Ammosova, 8

❹ When the painting is dry, position a piece of clear plastic wrap over the painted glass in the art. With a marker, lightly trace the shape of the container on the plastic. Cut the plastic shape out with scissors. Draw very light glue lines directly on the container in the painting. Then gently pat the plastic onto the glue lines, covering the clear container in the painting. The plastic will add shine to the glass!

Art Challenge

Try to paint what is seen in the clear container.
- The shape of the glass container
- The shape of what is inside the container
- The pattern of the tablecloth seen through the glass
- Reflections in the container

Watercolor Lesson

Begin with the lightest colors first, gradually painting darker areas next. It is always possible to paint things darker, but nearly impossible to paint things lighter.

Julian Schnabel

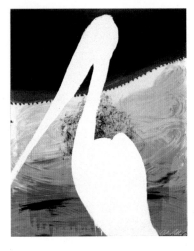

Julian Schnabel | *Guiseppe "brooding on the vast abyss,"* 1998
Hand-painted, 45 × 36 in, Courtesy of the artist and Lococo Fine Art, St. Louis. All rights reserved.

October 26, 1951–
Neo-Expressionist painter, Filmmaker

Julian Schnabel [SCHNAW-bel] is an American artist and filmmaker born in Brooklyn, New York. When Schnabel was very young, he and his family moved to Texas, where he would later attend the University of Houston and begin his art career. Schnabel is a major figure in the movement called Neo-Expressionism, art that is daring, emotional, and energetic. He is most famous for his large-scale "plate paintings" created on plates first smashed into many pieces and then glued to wooden panels. Also well known are his silhouetted shapes and forms over vivid backgrounds that are visually startling and tend to capture young artists' attention. Julian Schnabel is the father of five children, and he works in New York as well as at his summer home on Long Island. His artworks are in the collections of museums throughout the world.

Masked Form

From self-adhesive vinyl covering, cut a shape or form and gently press it on drawing paper. Paint a background with fingerpainting, spattering, or other energentic paint techniques, working right over the adhesive shape and over the paper. Peel the shape from the painting to see a silhouetted form in strong contrast to the unique background.

Materials

self-adhesive vinyl covering or contact paper
permanent marker or ballpoint pen
scissors
large drawing paper, any color

paints: fingerpaint, tempera paint, liquid watercolors, liquid starch, markers
tools: toothbrush, paintbrush, ruler, water, sponge

Process

❶ Draw a large bold shape on self-adhesive contact paper with the permanent marker or ballpoint pen. Draw it large enough to fill a good part of the paper. Then cut the shape out. Peel the protective covering away, and gently press the shape onto the drawing paper.

❷ Paint the paper in any chosen way, painting right over the shape. Some painting ideas include:
- Fingerpaint over the paper with a mixture of tempera paint and liquid starch. Use tools to drag designs through the paint or simply use fingers.
- To carefully splatter paint over the paper and shapes, pull a ruler over the bristles of a toothbrush (toward, not away). Splatter paint along the edges of the shape or over the entire paper.
- Slightly dampen the paper with a wet sponge. Paint with liquid watercolors or tempera paints on damp paper. Let the art dry fully before gently peeling the contact paper.
- Paint with full colors of tempera paint in any fashion.
- Draw over the paper with markers. Then paint the marker lines with plain water to bleed, blur, and smudge.
- Use any combination of techniques listed!

Happy Birthday Cake,
by Morgan Marshall, 6

❸ When the paint is slightly or completely dry, slowly and carefully peel away the contact paper shape from the paper. A clear, clean form will be left visible in the painted background. Choose to paint inside the empty form, or leave it untouched.

Websites to Explore

Internet Guidelines

The links suggested in this list offer websites checked by the authors to be safe and appropriate for young artists. From these, visit websites of the great museums and galleries from all over the world. However, websites change daily, and each site cannot be checked every day. We need your help. First, websites should be explored with parents or a supervising adult—always. An adult should preview the website before jumping in with kids. Being on the Internet is like visiting an unexplored planet—exciting and informative—but adults should hold children's hands for safety and guidance.

Great Online Art Museum Kid Sites

Some of the most famous museums in the world offer amazing kid sites where young artists can play games, create art, learn fun facts, or explore the world of art. Find special events and exhibits coming to museums and galleries in your area, or view special exhibits online. These links are some of the finest available for children.

Art as Experiment, Art as Experience
www.sfmoma.org/anderson/index.html
Interactive: featuring the works of Pollock, Stella, Rothko, Diebenkorn, de Kooning; "The Viewing Experience" and other activities for exploring Abstract Expressionist art.

Artist Biographies: Smithsonian American Art Museum, Washington, DC
americanart.si.edu/search/artist_biolist.cfm

Counting on Art: National Gallery of Art, Washington, DC
www.nga.gov/education/classroom/counting_on_art
Explore the paintings of Pippin and Thiebaud, and the mobiles of Calder—math and visual art concepts.

Destination-Modern Art: Museum of Modern Art, NY
www.moma.org/destination/#
A web movie for young kids from MOMA.

Eyes on Art: AT&T Art Education
www.kn.pacbell.com/wired/art2/quiz/index.html
Activities to help kids learn how to look at art.

Games and Activities: The Children's Museum of Indianapolis, IN
www.childrensmuseum.org/kids/games.htm
Games, events, exhibits, activities, newsletters, more.

Getty Games: Getty Museum, Los Angeles
www.getty.edu/gettygames/
Play online memory and puzzle games with the Getty.

Ghosts of the de Young: de Young Museum, San Francisco
www.thinker.org/fam/education/publications/ghost/index.html
Kids' cartoon tour of de Young Museum.

Making Sense of Modern Art: San Francisco Museum of Modern Art
www.sfmoma.org/MSoMA/index.html
"Zoom in" on full-screen details of individual artworks, explore excerpts from archival videos and films, and listen to commentary by artists, art historians, critics, and collectors.

Memento Mori: Tate Museum, Britain
www.tate.org.uk/kids/mementomori
Online art games from the Tate.

Metropolitan Museum of Art - Explore & Learn: Museum of Modern Art, New York
www.metmuseum.org/explore/index.asp

MOMA—Art Safari: Museum of Modern Art, New York
artsafari.moma.org

Sculpture Garden: National Gallery of Art, Washington, DC
www.nga.gov/kids/lizzy/overview_fst.htm
Animated tour of the Sculpture Garden.

NGA Kids: National Gallery of Art, Washington, DC
www.nga.gov/kids

Websites to Explore

Playground! Minneapolis Institute of Arts Walker Art Center, Minneapolis, Minnesota
www.artsconnected.org/playground/index.shtml

REMIX, Interactive Collage: Museum of Modern Art, NY
redstudio.moma.org/interactives/remix/index_f.html
Design photo-montage online, a site for high school kids.

Smithsonian American Art Museum Kids' Site: Smithsonian American Art Museum, Washington, DC
www.americanart.si.edu/index3.cfm

Tate Kids: The Tate Museum, UK
www.tate.org.uk/kids/

The Incredible Art Department
www.princetonol.com/groups/iad/
Art ideas, lessons, information. Links to website.

Learning at Whitney—The Kids' Gallery: Whitney Museum of American Art, New York
whitney.org/learning/gallery/
Accessible gallery of art—sorting and searching options.

Which Artists Share Your Birthday? Smithsonian American Art Museum, Washington, DC
americanart.si.edu/collections/interact/form/artist_birthdays.cfm

Great American Artists Websites

Learn about favorite artists and see their full-color artworks. Find out which galleries and exhibits might be in your area, and see the art in person.

Adams, Ansel
Official website: www.anseladams.com
Manzanar: memory.loc.gov/ammem/collections/anseladams/index.html
SFMOMA/100: www.sfmoma.org/adams/index.html

Asawa, Ruth
Official website: www.ruthasawa.com
Japanese American National Museum: www.janm.org/exhibits/asawa/activities

Audubon, John James
Official: www.audubon.org/bird/boa/BOA_index.html
NGA: www.nga.gov/collection/gallery/birdsam/birdsam-main1.html

Bearden, Romare
Official website: www.beardenfoundation.org
Met: www.metmuseum.org/explore/the_block/index_flash.html
Animated: www.sfmoma.org/bearden/index.html
The Cotton Pickers, interactive painting: www.bampfa.berkeley.edu

Bellows, George
Coloring page, NBMAA: www.nbmaa.org/edu/games/color.htm#
NGA: www.nga.gov/cgi-bin/pbio?2050

Benton, Thomas Hart
Smithsonian: americanart.si.edu/collections/tours/benton/index.html
Coloring page: www.nbmaa.org/edu/games/color.htm#

Biederman, Charles
Official website: www.charlesbiederman.net/gallery.html
Remembering Biederman: http://news.minnesota.publicradio.org/features/2004/12/28_ap_biedermanobit/

Borglum, Gutzon
Mount Rushmore: www.nps.gov/moru
PBS: www.pbs.org/wgbh/amex/rushmore/index.html

Buchanan, Beverly
Official website: www.beverlybuchanan.com

Calder, Alexander
Official website: www.calder.org
NGA: www.nga.gov/education/classroom/counting_on_art/bio_calder.shtm
NGA: www.nga.gov/exhibitions/calder/realsp/roomenter-foyer.htm
San Francisco MOMA: www.sfmoma.org/espace/calder/calder_intro.html

Cassatt, Mary
NGA: www.nga.gov/education/schoolarts/cassatt.shtm
Artchive: www.Artchive.com/Artchive/C/cassatt.html
WebMuseum: www.ibiblio.org/wm/paint/auth/cassatt/
Met: www.metmuseum.org/toah/hd/cast/hd_cast.htm

Catlett, Elizabeth
PBS: www.pbs.org/wnet/aaworld/arts/catlett.html
Images: www.mojoportfolio.com/artist_search/african_american/catlett.html
Art Institute of Chicago: www.artic.edu

Chihuly, Dale
Official website: www.chihuly.com/floats/selfloat.html
Children's Museum of Indianapolis: www.childrensmuseum.org

Close, Chuck
Official website: www.chuckclose.com
www.chuckclose.coe.uh.edu
MOMA: www.pbs.org/art21/artists/walker/index.html

Cooney, Barbara
Biography: www.ortakales.com/illustrators/Cooney.html
Horn Book: www.hbook.com
Chanticleer and the Fox: www.harpercollins.com

Copley, John S.
NGA: www.nga.gov/collection/gallery/gg60b/gg60b-main1.html
Watson and the Shark: www.nga.gov/kids/watson/watson1.htm
Met: www.metmuseum.org/explore/copley/copley.html, www.metmuseum.org/TOAH/HD/copl/hd_copl.htm

Cornell, Joseph
WebMuseum: www.ibiblio.org/wm/paint/auth/cornell
Smithsonian: americanart.si.edu/collections/interact/slideshow/cornell.cfm
Navigating the Imagination: www.pem.org/cornell

Currier & Ives
Gallery: currierandives.net

De Forest, Roy
Dog sculpture: www.dateline.ucdavis.edu
MOCFA: www.mocfa.org/exhibitions/06_animals/gallery1.htm
Smithsonian interview: www.aaa.si.edu

De Kooning, Willem
hirshhorn.si.edu/collection/search.asp?Artist=Willem+de+Kooning
edu.warhol.org/pdf/dekooning_handout.pdf.

Demuth, Charles
The Figure 5 in Gold: www.wisdomportal.com/Christmas/Figure5InGold.html
Charles Demuth Museum: www.demuth.org/

Diebenkorn, Richard
Official website: www.richarddiebenkorn.net/
PBS: www.pbs.org/wgbh/sisterwendy/works/oce.html
Interview: www.aaa.si.edu

Dine, Jim
Guggenheim: www.guggenheim.org/exhibitions/past_exhibitions/dine/dine_bottom2.html

Websites to Explore

Disney, Walt
Disney: disney.go.com/disneyatoz/familymuseum/index.html
History of Disneyland: www.justdisney.com/disneyland/

Doolittle, Bev
www.greenwichworkshop.com/
www.bevdoolittle.net
www.powersource.com/gallery/bev/default.html
www.webagora.com.br/1/bdoolittle1.htm

Fish, Janet
www.stewartstewart.com/artists/fish_janet/
www. Artnet.com/artist/6229/janet-fish.html

Frankenthaler, Helen
Bio: www.stfrancis.edu/en/student/beatart/frank.htm

Fuller, Buckminster
B Fuller Institute: www.bfi.org/our_programs/who_is_buckminster_fuller
Tetrahedral kites: illuminations.nctm.org/LessonDetail.aspx?id=L639

Goldberg, Rube
Official website: www.rubegoldberg.com/

Haring, Keith
Official website: www.haring.com
Haring for Kids: www.haringkids.com

Hicks, Edward
www.artcyclopedia.com/artists/hicks_edward.html
Met: www.metmuseum.org/explore/AmericanFolk/Folk1.htm

Hofmann, Hans
Official website: www.hanshofmann.net
Interactive: www.bampfa.berkeley.edu/education/kidsguide/hofmann/
    hofmann.html
PBS: www.pbs.org/hanshofmann/index.html

Hopper, Edward
NGA: www.nga.gov/exhibitions/hopperinfo.shtm

Smithsonian: americanart.si.edu/collections/exhibits/hopper/index.htm
Met: www.metmuseum.org/toah/hd/hopp/hd_hopp.htm

Indiana, Robert
Smithsonian: americanart.si.edu/education/cappy/14aindianabio.html
Postal Museum: www.postalmuseum.si.edu/artofthestamp/subpage%20
    table%20images/artwork/Artist%20Bios/robertindiana.htm

James, Jewell
www.ebuynativeart.com/Jewell/index.htm
Lummi Healing Poles: www.lummihealingpole.org

Jefferson, Thomas
Designs: concise.britannica.com/ebc/art-5454/The-rotunda-University-
    of-Virginia-Charlottesville-Va
Architect: xroads.virginia.edu/~cap/jeff/jeffarch.html
Plans: diagrams.org/fig-pages/f00003.html

Johns, Jasper
Met: www.metmuseum.org/toah/hd/john/hd_john.htm
PBS: www.pbs.org/wnet/americanmasters/database/johns_j.html
MOMA: www.moma.org/exhibitions/1996/johns/

Kahn, Wolf
Official website: www.wolfkahn.com
PBS: www.pbs.org/hanshofmann/wolf_kahn_001.html

Lichtenstein, Roy
Official website: www.lichtensteinfoundation.org
Kid Tales - Wham! www.princetonol.com/groups/iad/

Lin, Maya
PBS: www.pbs.org/art21/artists/lin/index.html
Profile: www.achievement.org/autodoc/page/lin0int-1

Magee, Alan
Official website: www.allenmagee.com

Martin, Agnes
Gallery: studiocleo.com/gallerie/martin/martin.html
Artcyclopedia: www.artcyclopedia.com/artists/martin_agnes.html
Harwood Museum: harwoodmuseum.org/gallery4.php?tag=about

Martínez, Maria
Pueblo Potter: www.thesantafesite.com
Bio: www.adobegallery.com/artist.php?artist_id=109
Family: www.mariajulianpottery.com/MariaMartinezBio.html
Black-on-black pottery: www.mariapottery.com

Moses, Grandma
Art: www.gseart.com/exh/exh_invt.asp?ExhID=480
www.benningtonmuseum.com
Gallery: www.gseart.com/moses.html

Neiman, LeRoy
Official website: www.leroyneiman.com
Art: www.asama.org/awards/sportArtists/artist2007.asp

O'Keeffe, Georgia
O'Keeffe Museum: www.okeeffemuseum.org
Art: www.artst.org/okeefe
Met: www.metmuseum.org/toah/hd/geok/hd_geok.htm
PBS: www.pbs.org/wnet/americanmasters/database/okeeffe_g.html

Oldenburg, Claes, and van Bruggen, Coosje
Official website: www.oldenburgvanbruggen.com
Met: www.metmuseum.org
Bio, artwork, links: www.pacewildenstein.com

Osorio, Pepón
Gallery: www.feldmangallery.com/pages/artistsrffa/artoso01.html
PBS: www.pbs.org/art21/artists/osorio/

Pierce, Elijah
Bio: www.shortnorth.com/PierceCoverStory.html
Bio: www.cscc.edu/ElijahPierce/bio.htm
Book of Wood: www.columbusmuseum.org/about/curatorsview/pierce.html

Pippin, Horace
NGA: www.nga.gov/kids/watson/watson1.htm
Explore History: www.explorepahistory.com/displaygallery.php?gallery_id=8&bcolor=ggreen&list=1
World War I Diary: www.aaa.si.edu/search/index.cfm/fuseaction/Items.ViewImageDetails/ItemID/7434

Pollock, Jackson
Interactive: www.jacksonpollock.org
Bio: naples.cc.sunysb.edu/CAS/PKHouse.nsf/pages/pollock
inks: wwar.com/masters/p/pollock-jackson.html

Powers, Harriet
www.artcyclopedia.com/artists/powers_harriet.html
xroads.virginia.edu/~ug97/quilt/harriet.html
www.earlywomenmasters.net/powers/index.html
www.historyofquilts.com/hpowers.html
Met: www.metmuseum.org/toah/hd/amqc/hd_amqc.htm

Raffael, Joseph
Official website: www.josephraffael.com
Gallery: www.nancyhoffmangallery.com/artists/raffael.html
MMOCA: www.mmoca.org/mmocacollects/artist_page.php?id=24

Remington, Frederic
Frederic Remington Museum: www.fredericremington.org
Met: www.metmuseum.org/toah/hd/bsaw/hd_bsaw.htm
Musselman Museum: www.gettysburg.edu/library/news/special_events/onebook/2006/exhibits/remingtons/index.html

Ringgold, Faith
Official website: www.faithringgold.com
Peace Story Quilt: www.inter-relations.org/quilt.htm
PBS: www.pbs.org/wnet/aaworld/arts/ringgold.html

Websites to Explore

Rockwell, Norman
Official website: www.normanrockwell.com
Norman Rockwell Museum: www.nrm.org
Saturday Evening Post covers: www.nrm.org/page140

Rothko, Mark
NGA: www.nga.gov/feature/rothko/
Rothko website: www.nga.gov/feature/rothko/intro1.html
www.thecityreview.com/rothko.html

Sargent, John Singer
Met: www.metmuseum.org/toah/hd/sarg/hd_sarg.htm
Smithsonian: americanart.si.edu/collections/tours/sargent/index.html
www.dl.ket.org/Webmuseum/wm/paint/auth/sargent/index.htm

Schnabel, Julian
Gallery: www.lococofineart.com

Scholder, Fritz
Bio: www.scholder.com/scholder_bio.html
Bio: www.bbhc.org/wgwa/scholder.cfm
Profile: www.achievement.org/autodoc/page/sch1pro-1
Art: scholder.com/paintings01.html

Seuss, Dr. (Theodor S. Geisel)
Seussville: www.seussville.com
Art: www.drseussart.com

Skoglund, Sandy
Official website: www.sandyskoglund.com

Steinberg, Saul
Official website: www.saulsteinbergfoundation.org
New Yorker art: www.cartoonbank.com

Stella, Frank
NGA game: www.nga.gov/kids/stella/stella1.htm
PBS: www.pbs.org/hanshofmann/frank_stella_001.html

Stuart, Gilbert
Met: www.metmuseum.org/explore/gilbert_stuart/index.html
Met: www.metmuseum.org/toah/hd/stua/hd_stua.htm

Thiebaud, Wayne
NGA: www.nga.gov/education/classroom/counting_on_art/bio_thiebaud.shtm
Smithsonian: www.aaa.si.edu/exhibits/pastexhibits/thiewayn/thiebaud.htm

Tiffany, Louis C.
Met: www.metmuseum.org/explore/Tiffany/index.html
Met: www.metmuseum.org/toah/hd/tiff/hd_tiff.htm

Walker, Kara
PBS: www.pbs.org/art21/artists/walker/index.html
learn.walkerart.org/karawalker
SFMOMA: www.sfmoma.org/msoma/artworks/8417.html

Warhol, Andy
Warhol Museum: edu.warhol.org
Warhol Foundation: www.warholfoundation.org
PBS: www.pbs.org/wnet/americanmasters/database/warhol_a.html

Whistler, James M.
Whistler House Museum: www.whistlerhouse.org
Bio: www.glyphs.com/art/whistler/

Wood, Grant
ARTIC: www.artic.edu/artaccess/AA_Modern/pages/MOD_5.shtml
americanart.si.edu/collections/interact/gallery/wood.cfm
xroads.virginia.edu/~MA98/haven/wood/home.html

Wright, Frank Lloyd
Frank Lloyd Wright Foundation: www.franklloydwright.org
PBS: www.pbs.org/flw/
Met: www.metmuseum.org/toah/hd/flwt/hd_flwt.htm
Architect Studio: architectstudio3d.org/AS3d/design_studio.html

Glossary

New words and ideas are explored throughout this book. Brief explanations, definitions, and descriptions are offered to help answer questions, clearly describe terms, and give examples of artists who fit the term.

abstract   art that is geometric in design or simplified from its natural appearance; abstract art does not need to look like anything real.

Abstract Expressionism   an artistic movement from 1930 to 1960 stressing spontaneity and individuality, and featuring abstract designs. Helen Frankenthaler, Mark Rothko, Willem de Kooning, and Richard Diebenkorn are Abstract Expressionists. Interpretations are highly imaginary.

action painting   a painting method that uses movement to fling or throw paint onto the canvas. Jackson Pollock is the best known American action artist.

acrylic   a kind of paint that uses a liquid plastic base. Acrylics dissolve in water when wet, but not after the paint dries.

appliqué   a type of fiber art in which pieces of fabric are stuck or sewn onto a background fabric to create a design or picture. Harriet Powers created appliqués on her quilts.

arch   a curved structure that spans an opening in a wall, often creating a window or passageway. A stone arch is built of shaped stones, with a keystone at the top of the curve that locks the whole structure together. Thomas Jefferson used the arch in his building designs.

architect   a person who designs and creates buildings, houses, and structures. Wright, Jefferson, and Lin are architects.

Arts & Crafts   a style of decorative arts at the turn of the 20th century, 1880–1910. Frank Lloyd Wright's architecture is part of the Arts & Crafts movement.

art elements   the visual components that artists use to create, such as shape, texture, space, line, and color.

art medium   materials used in creating an art work; examples are paint, crayon, paper, clay, wire, and so on.

Art Nouveau   a style of art popular around 1900. Designs were often made out of natural forms such as leaves, vines, and flowers. Louis Comfort Tiffany's glass art is part of the Art Nouveau movement.

Ashcan School   a group of American painters of the early 20th century who painted realistic scenes of everyday city life. They got the name "ashcan" because they chose to paint pictures of poor people and neighborhoods, rather than scenes of beauty and grandeur. Examples are George Bellows and Edward Hopper.

assemblage   an art process where three-dimensional materials are joined together to build up an art work. Joseph Cornell's boxes are assemblage.

bas relief   a kind of sculpture in which objects stick up slightly from the background. Asawa and Pierce created bas relief sculptures.

block print   a kind of printmaking in which a design is carved into a block of solid material, such as wood or linoleum.

brayer   a small, handheld roller used to spread ink or paint onto a printmaking block.

bronze   a metal made of copper and tin, used in casting sculptures. Remington and Asawa sculptures were reproduced in bronze.

canvas   a strong fabric stretched over a wood frame to paint on; often refers to any surface on which paintings are created.

cartoonist   an artist who creates cartoon characters, comics, and animations. Saul Steinberg is a cartoonist.

casting   a method of making three-dimensional sculptures by pouring a hardening liquid or melted material into a mold with that impression. Frederic Remington created sculptures using casting.

center of interest   in a painting, objects, colors, and designs can be placed in a way to draw the eye to one area of interest in the work.

ceramic   pottery art; works of clay glazed and then baked in a kiln.

charcoal   a soft drawing material traditionally made out of burnt wood.

clay   an art material found in the earth that can be purchased, sometimes called moist clay or earth clay; may also refer to other modeling compounds such as Plasticine, Sculpey, or Fimo, which are used like clay but are not an earth clay.

collaboration   two or more people working together to create a piece of art. Dale Chihuly directs a team of artists in building collaborative glass art. Claes Oldenburg and Coosje van Bruggen collaborated on super-size sculptures.

Glossary

collage   artwork made by cutting up various materials such as string, fabric, newspaper, photos, cardboard, bits of paintings and drawings, and putting them together with glue or other bonding material. A collage can also be called a montage. Faith Ringgold and Romare Bearden are collage artists.

Color Field   a style of American abstract painting, 1940–1970, where large, simple areas of solid color create the image.

chalk   an art material made of talc and pigment pressed into sticks for coloring; some chalk is used on sidewalks or chalk boards; chalks for fine art are called pastels.

combine   a type of art similar to collage and assemblage, where a collection of objects or materials are combined to create a work of art. Pronounced CAHM-byn.

commercial artist   an artist who creates advertisements, posters, commercials, or other materials for promoting and selling products.

concept art   art in which the idea or story being expressed is the reason for the artwork. Bev Doolittle calls herself a concept artist.

Constructionist   an art style that integrates math and geometry with art and design. Charles Biederman is a Constructionist.

contemporary   the present time; a term used to describe an artist who is living and creating in the present time.

contraption   a sculpture or art work that is similar to an invention and may or may not have any use, usually overdone in scope and presentation; can be filled with imaginary details. Rube Goldberg's drawings show imaginary contraptions.

Cubist   the first abstract art style of the 20th century. Instead of art that was realistic or representational, art was expressed with neutral color and geometric form. Hans Hofmann's earlier work is Cubist.

cylinder   a three-dimensional form that is like a rounded tube or pipe in any variety of dimensions, heights, and widths.

Dada   an art movement in the early 1900s. Dada artists often poked fun at the seriousness of traditional art and created works that were meant to be absurd and outrageous.

design   the plan or arrangement of a work of art.

diptych   two panels hinged together to create a larger piece of art. Joseph Raffael often paints diptychs.

earthenware   pottery made out of clay dug from the earth, then fired or baked until hard; terra cotta is type of unglazed reddish earthenware used for sculpture, pottery, and as a building material.

environment   all of the surroundings, climate, or habitat of one particular area; in art, sometimes considered a scene that is painted with all its details.

environmental art (land art)   art created out of natural objects, especially in natural outdoor settings. Robert Smithson created monumental land art in the outdoor environment.

expression   the interpretation of inner emotion, vision, or strong feeling.

Expressionism   a style of art in which reality is distorted with the expression of the artists' inner emotions and visions; emotional impact is created with strong colors, abstract forms, and bold brushstrokes. The first expressionist art began in the early 1900s. Georgia O'Keeffe and LeRoy Nieman are Expressionists. Also see *Abstract Expressionism* and *Neo-Expressionists*.

Fauvism   a style of painting in the early 1900s characterized by pictures made with strong colors and simple shapes.

fiber art   art that is made from cloth, fabric, string, rope, or other natural fibers. Harriet Powers and Faith Ringgold are fiber artists because they work with fabric and quilting.

filmmaker   an artist who makes movies. Julian Schnabel is a filmmaker.

folk art   works of art that are used in everyday life, created by people that are not professionally trained in art. Grandma Moses and Horace Pippin were folk artists.

Funk Art   a group of artists in 1960–1970 who created artworks by combining found objects and junk with traditional sculpture and painting materials. Roy De Forest was a Funk Artist.

geodesic dome   a geometric form made out of short sections of lightweight material joined into interlocking polygons. Buckminster Fuller's geodesic dome is an important invention in modern architecture.

geometric designs   artworks created with geometric shapes, such as a square, circle, rectangle, triangle, as well as cube, sphere, pyramid, or cylinder, as the primary form of the creation.

glass artist an artist working with glass, such as glassblowers and stained glass artists. Dale Chihuly, Louis Comfort Tiffany, and Frank Lloyd Wright are glass artists.

glassblowing the process of shaping glass into useful shapes when hot glass is in a molten, liquid state. Dale Chihuly creates glass globes or balls in this fashion.

graffiti words, letters, and images that people paint or draw on public surfaces, such as buildings, walls, and railroad cars. Keith Haring began his career with chalk graffiti in the New York subways.

graphic artist a person who illustrates or designs with a pictorial technique; not interpretive as much as measured and precise; often incorporates and redesigns the art of others through photography and computer techniques. Alan Magee began his career as a graphic artist.

Harlem Renaissance the name given to a group of African American artists who worked in New York City from 1920–1940. Romare Bearden was part of this movement.

horizon the line seen where the sky and the land come together; the word horizontal comes from this term.

illustrator an artist who creates pictures for books, magazines, and advertisements. Barbara Cooney and Norman Rockwell were illustrators.

image any picture, drawing, sculpture, photograph, or other form that creates a likeness or representation of an object.

imagination a particularly human trait of being able to think up ideas and dreams and transform them into art.

Impressionism a major movement and new way of creating art in the late 1800s; painters used natural, free brushwork and painted sunlight into their colors; often showed an impression of reality rather than a perfect lifelike report of the subject. Mary Cassatt is the most famous American Impressionist.

installation a work of art that is built in a three-dimensional gallery space. Kara Walker, Sandy Skoglund, and Pépon Osorio create installations.

interior design the art of designing and decorating rooms and other spaces inside buildings.

inventor a person who thinks up a new and better way to do something, designs, and often constructs that idea. Buckminster Fuller was an inventor.

junk items usually thrown away, but in the case of art, collected for uses such as collage, sculpture, assemblage, and other kinds of art. Joseph Cornell included junk in his art boxes.

keystone arch an arch used in building that has one central supporting stone holding the arch in place. Thomas Jefferson often used the keystone arch in his building designs.

kiln an extremely hot oven for baking clay to a hard and permanent result.

Kitsch Art art that is sentimental or a superficial imitation of real art. Contemporary artists like Pépon Osorio create kitsch art as an intentional cultural statement.

Land Art also called *Earth Art*; a form of sculpture in which landforms are altered or shaped. Robert Smithson created Land Art.

landscape an art work where the features of the land are the most important subject; usually trees, mountains, rivers, sky, countryside, and so on.

lithograph a method of printmaking. Currier & Ives prints were lithographs.

mask a mask is a material that covers and blocks out part of the art image and is later removed to reveal what's underneath.

mat board sometimes spelled *matte board*; a useful, versatile, heavy paper board; available in scraps in a variety of colors and textures; saved from picture frame shops; useful in children's art; can be purchased in large sheets.

mixed media the use of two or more art mediums in an art work; for example, an art work where crayon, paint, and chalk are all used together.

medium the material and technique used to create a work of art.

Minimalism a style of art, 1950–1990, which used simple and very subtle shapes and colors. Agnes Martin was a minimalist.

mobile a sculpture that balances and hangs from the ceiling or from a stand. Alexander Calder created hanging sculptures, and along with the Dada artist Marcel Duchamp, invented the word "mobile" from the French words for movement and intention.

Glossary

modeling compound any of the clays or playclays, including earth clay and playclay, Plasticine, Fimo, and Sculpey.

mold a hollow shape that is filled with a material that hardens, creating a piece of art.

mono one; monochrome is one color or tone and monoprint is one image or print.

monoprint when one print is made from one image, rather than many prints from one image. Mary Cassatt made monoprints.

monument a memorial, gravestone, or statue to help others remember a person, group of people, important happening, or part of history that is in the past. Gutzon Borglum's Mount Rushmore and Maya Lin's Vietnam Wall are memorials.

mosaic a type of surface decoration used on walls, tables, and walkways. Little bits of colored stone or glass are pressed into cement making a design or pattern; in children's art, often refers to less permanent art works made with paper, beans and seeds, egg shells, or other materials.

mural a large painting, often painted on a wall; sometimes painted by more than one person; may be a painting on large canvas or wood panels attached to a wall. Thomas Hart Benton painted murals.

muslin a pure cotton fabric, usually beige or white, such as a bed sheet.

narrative an artwork that tells a story. Norman Rockwell, Grandma Moses, and Bev Doolittle are narrative artists.

Naturalism realistic representation in art; the practice of reproducing subjects as exactly as possible. John James Audubon was a naturalist.

negative shape the background shapes that surround the main positive shapes of a work of art.

Neo-Expressionism 1970s to mid-1980s; a term often used for contemporary or modern paintings in the Expressionist style. Neo-Expressionists were sometimes called New Fauves.

observe to look closely; in art, to notice details and record them.

onomatopoeia the formation or use of words such as buzz or VAROOM that imitate the sounds associated with the object or action referred to. Lichtenstein used words like this in his paintings in comic form.

palette any board or tray on which colors are mixed; also refers to the selection of colors an artist chooses to paint an art work.

pastel chalk soft art chalks in many colors.

pastels, oil a crayon made of ground color (pigments) and mixed with a sticky water or oil; or a drawing made with these coloring sticks.

pattern in art a pattern usually means to repeat a design; a pattern can be a single design or stencil that is traced.

performance art a piece of art in which people play a part, acting out planned events as viewers watch.

perspective a painting or drawing with images and objects that produce an impression of distance and size.

photography the art of using a camera and film to capture images; can be expressive or realistic; useful for portraits, landscapes, and all other forms of picture-taking. Ansel Adams and Sandy Skoglund are photographers.

photojournalism using the art of photography to capture a story, tell a story, or impart history, such as Ansel Adams's Manzanar photos.

photomontage a type of collage made mostly of photographs. Romare Bearden created photomontages.

Photorealism a style of art based on an ultrarealistic representation of the subject.

pigment the part of paint that is the color; mix pigment with egg, water, or other liquid; pigment comes from natural things such as the earth, insects, flowers, or can be manufactured.

playclay a non-hardening oil-base modeling medium; sometimes called Plasticine.

polymer clay a plastic-based clay such as Fimo or Sculpey that can be baked hard or reused over and over if not baked; comes in many colors and is highly malleable.

Polystyrene as in the "grocery tray," a handy material often saved for use in children's art; used for containers for art supplies; foods can be purchased on these trays from grocery stores; come in black, gray, and most often in white, in many shapes and sizes.

Pop Art   an art form started in the 1950s and 1960s that used American mass culture and everyday commercial images from foods, cars, and famous people. Two great Pop artists are Roy Lichtenstein (based his artwork on comic strips, advertising, and bubble-gum wrappers) and Andy Warhol (showed soup can labels and movie stars in repetition). Many Pop artists, including Wayne Thiebaud and Claes Oldenburg, have continued to expand their works into contemporary styles.

portrait   a painting or drawing of a person, sometimes the head and shoulders only, other times the entire body.

Post-Abstract Expressionism   a style of art since the mid-1900s combining the pure designs of Abstract Expressionism with greater reality. Jasper Johns is a Post-Abstract Expressionist.

poster paint   a type of tempera paint. Use poster paint or tempera paint when tempera paint is called for.

pottery   pots, cups, vases, urns, and other containers made from clay and baked hard in a kiln or other oven. Maria Martínez created black-on-black pottery

Precisionism   a style of art in the early 1900s combining Realism with geometric design. Growing out of the Cubist movement, American Precisionists include Charles Demuth and the early works of Georgia O'Keeffe.

primary colors   the basic colors from which all other colors can be made; the primary colors are red, blue, and yellow; mixed in varying ways, these make other colors like green, orange, purple, and so on.

printmaking   art techniques that involve taking a print of a design, texture, or image with paint, ink, or other art mediums and then pressing it onto another material such as paper to capture the image. Mary Cassatt used printmaking to make monoprints.

profile   a picture of something seen from the side, like the side view of a person's face.

quilter   a fiber artist who stitches small pieces of cloth together to create a blanket or coverlet. Harriet Powers made quilts with appliqué designs. Faith Ringgold creates art that incorporates quilting.

Realism   a style of art in which artists show life as it really is, rather than an ideal or romantic view. Early American artists like Audubon and Remington were Realists, portraying their subjects in truthful detail. The Ashcan School artists of the early 1900s, like George Bellows, were Realists. Realism is also an important movement in Contemporary Art. Often called Photorealism, artists like Alan Magee create realist artwork.

realistic   when something in art is created to look real, just like it does in actual life.

Regionalism   the name given in the early 1900s to artwork from rural areas; artists who painted images from their own regions. Thomas Hart Benton and Grant Wood are American Regionalists.

relief   a sculpture or printmaking block with parts that stick out from the background.

Romantic   a style of art in the late 1800s emphasizing emotionalism, idealism, and inspiring scenes. The company of Currier & Ives printed romantic scenes.

scratchboard   an art material made from claycoated board on which black ink is applied. Lines and areas are scratched or scraped into the black surface with sharp-edged tools, revealing the white or colored board beneath.

sculptor   an artist who creates sculptures (see *sculpture*).

sculpture   an art form that is three-dimensional, made from any materials, and is usually freestanding.

self-portrait   a drawing or painting made by the artist of himself or herself.

series   artworks that connect in their subject or design and are meant to be viewed together, or go together in order.

shading   a gradual change from light to dark. Shading is one way to create the feeling of depth and three dimensions in an artwork.

silhouette   an outline-style drawing filled in with one color; a shadow or single shape against a background. Kara Walker and Julian Schnabel use silhouettes in their art.

soak stain   a technique where paint is poured, rather than brushed, onto canvas or paper to create fields of color. Helen Frankenthaler is a well-known soak stain artist.

Glossary

stabile   a sculpture with parts that are designed to move. Alexander Calder created both stabiles and mobiles (sculptures that hang from the ceiling).

stained glass   pieces of colored glass joined together with a material such as lead to form a design. Frank Lloyd Wright and Louis Comfort Tiffany created stained-glass windows.

still life   objects placed in an arrangement as the subject of a painting. Janet Fish creates still life paintings.

straight edge   any material or object that can be used like a ruler and has a completely straight edge, such as a piece of plastic, the edge of a book, or a paint-stirring stick.

Styrofoam   white packing material (a byproduct of petroleum), very lightweight and found in many shapes and textures.

Surrealism   art expressed by fantastic imaginary thoughts and images, often expressing dreams and subconscious thoughts as part of reality; illogical and unexpected, surprising imaginary art. Sandy Skoglund's photographs of her installations are surreal.

symmetry   balance or regularity of two sides; one half of something is exactly like the other half.

tableau   a group of models or motionless figures creating a scene. Sandy Skoglund creates tableau installations that she photographs.

tag signature   a unique, individual design that a graffiti artist uses to sign artwork. Keith Haring's tag signature is a crawling baby with radiating lines.

talk balloon   a cloud shape next to a character in a cartoon or comic where the words of the character are written to show the character is talking; can be used with inanimate images like a box or a mountain as examples, as well as with people, animals, or creatures. Roy Lichtenstein often painted talk balloons or sound balloons in his comic-style artworks.

technique   a method or procedure for making art; some common art techniques for children are crayon resist, wet-on-wet painting, and brushed chalk.

tempera paint   a common art material found in schools and homes; available in liquid or powdered forms and in many colors; ground pigments sometimes mixed with egg or oil.

texture   the quality of the surface of a work of art; for example, rough or smooth; the texture can be felt, seen, or both.

theme park   an amusement park built around one unifying idea or topic, such as cartoon characters, movies, or science fiction. Walt Disney designed many theme parks.

three-dimensional (3-D)   artwork that is solid and has all dimensions: height, width, and depth; not flat; applies to sculptures or works that stand up from a flat surface. Oldenburg & van Bruggen create large scale 3-D sculptures.

trace   place a thin sheet of paper or other material over an art work and draw over it, making the same design or image.

Traditional Art   artworks that adhere to cultural styles that have been used for centuries, such as Native American pottery by Maria Martínez and Pacific Northwest carvings by Jewell James.

wash   a thin, watery mixture of paint, often used over a crayon drawing to resist the crayon and absorb only into the paper; used in watercolor painting, brush drawing, and occasionally in oil painting to describe a thin layer of paint or ink.

watercolor   thin, transparent, water-soluble paint; comes in children's watercolor boxes, in squeeze tubes, and in dry blocks; when mixed with water, it thins, and is used as paint.

waterscape, seascape, or oceanscape   a work of art in which water is the main subject, such as the ocean, the sea, or other bodies of water.

wet-on-wet painting   a painting technique where wet paint is applied to wet paper.

wood cut, wood print, wood block   a print made by cutting a design in a block of wood and printing only the raised surfaces (not the cut-in areas) on paper. Elizabeth Catlett creates prints from wood blocks.

Artists by Art Style

Abstract Minimalist painter
Agnes Martin
Frank Philip Stella

Abstract sculptor
Alexander Calder

Architect
Buckminster Fuller
Thomas Jefferson
Maya Lin

Architect, Glass artist
Frank Lloyd Wright

Abstract Expressionist painter
Willem de Kooning
Richard Diebenkorn
Helen Frankenthaler
Hans Hofmann
Wolf Kahn
Jackson Pollock
Mark Rothko

Post-Abstract Expressionist painter
Jasper Johns
LeRoy Neiman

Cartoonist, Illustrator
Rube Goldberg
Saul Steinberg

Concept painter
Bev Doolittle

Constructionist sculptor
Charles Biederman

Expressionist painter
Georgia O'Keeffe

Expressionist painter, Photomontage
Romare Bearden

Expressionist sculptor
Ruth Asawa

Neo-Expressionist painter
Julian Schnabel
Fritz Scholder

Fiber artist, quilter, sculptor
Faith Ringgold
Harriet Powers

Folk Art painter
Edward Hicks
Grandma Moses

Folk Art sculptor
Beverly Buchanan
Elijah Pierce

Folk Art fiber artist
Harriet Powers

Folk Art Illustrator
Barbara Cooney
Horace Pippin

Funk Art sculptor, painter
Roy De Forest

Glass artist
Dale Chihuly
Louis Comfort Tiffany
Frank Lloyd Wright

Graffiti artist, graphic artist
Keith Haring

Illustrator, children's book
Barbara Cooney
Theodor Seuss Geisel

Illustrator, Romantic
Norman Rockwell
Currier & Ives

Impressionist painter, printmaker
Mary Cassatt

Installation, Glass artist
Dale Chihuly

Installation, Kitsch sculptor
Pepon Osorio

Installation, Silhouette artist
Kara Walker

Land Art sculptor
Robert Smithson

Naturalist
John James Audubon

Minimalist (Abstract) painter
Agnes Martin
Frank Philip Stella

Photorealist painter
Chuck Close

Artists by Style

 Photographer, Realist
Ansel Adams
Photographer, Surreal
Sandy Skoglund

 Pop Art painter
Robert Indiana
Roy Lichtenstein
Wayne Thiebaud
Andy Warhol
Pop Art painter, sculptor
Jim Dine
Pop Art sculptor
Oldenberg & van Bruggen

 Potter, traditional native Southwest
Maria Martínez

 Precisionist painter
Charles Demuth

 Printmaker, sculptor
Elizabeth Catlett
Printmaker, illustrator
Currier & Ives

 Realist painter
Janet Fish
Edward Hopper
Alan Magee
James McNeill Whistler
William Sidney Mount
John Singer Sargent
Realist painter, Ashcan School
George Bellows
Realist painter, Contemporary
Joseph Raffael
Realist painter, Naturalist, illustrator
John James Audubon
Realist painter, Portrait
Gilbert Stuart
Realist painter, Portrait, Narrative
John Singleton Copley
Realist painter, sculptor
Frederic Remington
Realist photographer
Ansel Adams
Realist sculptor
Gutzon Borglum

 Regional Expressionist sculptor
Beverly Buchanan
Regionalist painter
Thomas Hart Benton
Grant Wood

 Romantic illustrator
Norman Rockwell
Romantic illustrator, printmaker
Currier & Ives

 Surrealist, assemblage sculptor
Joseph Cornell
Surrealist, installation photography
Sandy Skoglund

 Theme Park designer, animator
Walt Disney

 Wood Carver
Elijah Pierce
Wood Carver, traditional native Pacific Northwest
Jewell James

Portrait Credits

John Singleton Copley, p. 2, by Madeline VandeHoef, 8
Thomas Jefferson, p. 4, by Kellie Fiebig, 11
Gilbert Stuart, p. 5, by Sammie VanLoo, 8
Edward Hicks, p. 6, by Lorenzo Ramos, 9
John James Audubon, p. 8, by Feliciano Paulino-Tellez, 10
Frederic Remington, p. 10, by Cedar Kerwin, 12
Mary Cassatt, p. 12, by Tara Gartner, 11
Harriet Powers, p. 14, by Devin Gartner, 9
Nathaniel Currier and James Ives, p. 15, by Tore Olson, 10
Louis Comfort Tiffany, p. 16, by Cedar Kirwin, 14
James McNeill Whistler, p. 18, by Molly Brandt, 13
John Singer Sargent, p. 19, by Lorenzo Ramos, 9
William Sidney Mount, p. 20, by Kellie Fiebig, 11
Edward Hopper, p. 22, by Kelly Klem, 10
Frank Lloyd Wright, p. 24, by Eric Klem, 12
Gutzon Borglum, p. 26, by Madeline VandeHoef, 8
Grandma Moses, p. 27, by Abbi Garcia, 10
Hans Hofmann, p. 28, by Alexander Petersen, 9
Charles Demuth, p. 29, by Madeline VandeHoef, 8
George Bellows, p. 30, by Sierra Smith, 7
Joseph Cornell, p. 32, by Laura Klem, 9
Maria Martínez, p. 34, by Tara Gartner, 11
Elijah Pierce, p. 35, by Andy Brandt, 9
Horace Pippin, p. 36, by Molly Brandt, 13
Thomas Hart Benton, p. 38, by Davis Bode, 9
Rube Goldberg, p. 39, by Sierra Smith, 7
Grant Wood, p. 40, by Amanda Warner, 11
Norman Rockwell, p. 42, by Abby Brandt, 11
Ansel Adams, p. 44, by Sean Helligso, 11
Alexander Calder, p. 46, by Sammie VanLoo, 8
Walt Disney, p. 47, by Alexandra Schulhauser, 10
Charles Biederman, p. 48, by Sammie VanLoo, 8
Mark Rothko, p. 50, by Alexander Petersen, 9
Willem de Kooning, p. 51, by Tonimarie Costanzo, 9
Barbara Cooney, p. 52, by Kaleeyah Stauffer, 7
Buckminster Fuller, p. 54, by Sammie VanLoo, 8
Jackson Pollock, p. 56, by Kaiden VanDalen, 8

Saul Steinberg, p. 57, by Sammie VanLoo, 8
Romare Bearden, p. 58, by Carson Bode, 7
Theodor Seuss Geisel, p. 60, by Sierra Smith, 7
Wolf Kahn, p. 62, by Jayme Elliott-Workman, 11
Richard Diebenkorn, p. 64, by Julia Odegaard, 10
Jasper Johns, p. 66, by Alexander Petersen, 9
Andy Warhol, p. 67, by Eric Klem, 12
Wayne Thiebaud, p. 68, by Tori Crabtree, 8
Roy Lichtenstein, p. 70, by Kennedy Perry, 7
Robert Indiana, p. 72, by Treyton Brewer, 7
Ruth Asawa, p. 74, by Madeline VandeHoef, 8
Helen Frankenthaler, p. 76, by Cameron Bol, 8
Agnes Martin, p. 77, by Emily Clark, 9
Elizabeth Catlett, p. 78, by BreAuna Phair, 8
Georgia O'Keeffe, p. 79, by Cedar Kirwin, 12
LeRoy Neiman, p. 80, by Carson Bode, 7
Claes Oldenburg and Coosje van Bruggen, p. 82, by Abby Brandt, 11
Keith Haring, p. 84, by Amanda Warner, 11
Robert Smithson, p. 86, by Morgan Van Slyke, 12
Roy De Forest, p. 88, by Irina Ammosova, 8
Fritz Scholder, p. 90, by BreAuna Phair, 8
Sandy Skoglund, p. 91, by McKenzie Thompson, 8
Joseph Raffael, p. 92, by Brett Bovenkamp, 8
Faith Ringgold, p. 94, by Bryonna Mobley, 11
Jim Dine, p. 96, by Carson Bode, 7
Frank Philip Stella, p. 97, by Sarah Klem, 7
Alan Magee, p. 98, by Jordan Holmstrom, 8
Chuck Close, p. 100, by Caleb Gish, 11
Jewell Praying Wolf James, p. 102, by Alexander Petersen, 9
Pepón Osorio, p. 103, by Cody, 8
Beverly Buchanan, p. 104, by Irina Ammosova, 8
Maya Lin, p. 105, by Cristina Hernandez, 8
Bev Doolittle, p. 106, by Maddison Fox, 8
Dale Chihuly, p. 108, by Abby Brandt, 11
Kara Walker, p. 110, by Sierra Smith, 7
Janet Fish, p. 112, by Eric Klem, 12
Julian Schnabel, p. 114, by Austin Cooper, 8

Index

Index

Index